W9-DIE-466

INDOOR Soccer!

by Klaas de Boer

Published by
Reedswain Inc.

Dedication

To the late Claudio Coutinho, who taught me the meaning of the word humility.

Photo Acknowledgements
Tim Rogers, *Public Relations Director, Cleveland Force*
Ken Garney, Mayfield Heights, Ohio
Glenn McGregor, Newark, Ohio

ISBN 1-890946-68-0
Library of Congress Control Number 2001093779
Copyright© 2001

All rights reserved. Except for use in a review.The reproduction or utilization of this book in any form or by any electronic, mechanical or other means, now known or hereafter invented, including xerography, photocopying and recording, and in any information storage and retrieval system, is forbidden without written permission of the publisher.

Printed by
DATA REPRODUCTIONS
Auburn, Michigan

Reedswain Publishing
612 Pughtown Road
Spring City, PA 19475
800.331.5191
www.reedswain.com
info@reedswain.com

About the author.....

Klaas de Boer (shown below, hand raised) is a leader in the development of America's newest, dynamic sport, indoor soccer. He was Assistant Coach with the Detroit Lightning of the Major Indoor Soccer League. In 1985 he led the Canton Invaders of the American Indoor Soccer Association to a 31-9 record and the first AISA championship. In that same year he was named coach of the year by the league. Currently, he is Head Coach and General Manager of the Toledo Pride of the American Indoor Soccer Association.

Holding a USSF "A" license and a former USSF Staff Coach, de Boer starred at Michigan State University, where they went to the National Championship final round. As a professional he played four seasons in the American Soccer League with Boston and with Cleveland. He was named Collegiate Coach of the Year in 1977 by the National Soccer Coaches Association, when he was at Cleveland State. He also assisted in coaching the Los Angeles Aztecs and Detroit Express in the North American Soccer League.

A Charter Member of several youth soccer leagues, he is Director of the Midwest Soccer Academy, one of the leading soccer camps in the United States.

TABLE OF CONTENTS

INTRODUCTION

Having been involved with outdoor soccer for most of my coaching career, I needed a quick introduction into the skills and tactics of indoor soccer when I accepted the coaching position of the Canton Invaders of the American Indoor Soccer Association. The 1984-85 season was its inaugural year. I had been involved with the Detroit Lightning of the Major Indoor Soccer League back in 1980, but most of my experience was with outdoor professional clubs. After doing considerable research, I came to the conclusion there is, in fact, very little information relating to coaching indoor soccer. I immediately immersed myself in a crash course of familiarizing myself with all aspects of the indoor game: formations, line changes, power plays, man down situations, and the use of the boards. Assistant Coach Jay Hoffman of the Cleveland Force helped me out initially by sharing some of his experience. I attended several professional hockey and basketball games to find out what I could learn from these sports. In addition I began to study indoor soccer games on videotape.

Finally Timo Liekoski of the Cleveland Force allowed me to attend several practice sessions with his team. This proved very beneficial in terms of organizing an indoor practice as well as in coming up with specific indoor drills and exercises. Best of all, I surrounded myself with a few MISL veterans like Don Tobin and Oscar Pisano, whose knowledge proved to be invaluable, particularly to the younger players with little if any indoor experience.

Even with all this preseason preparation, however, it was obvious to me I would have to learn the hard way... through on-the-job training. It was with nervous apprehension that I approached the opening game of the season against the Columbus Capitals. Dragan Popovic, former coach of the perennial MISL champion New York Arrows, has said coaching indoor soccer is like being a direct participant in the game. After the game you are mentally exhausted. I know what he means. The game against Columbus was a see-saw battle with Canton finally pulling it out by scoring the winning goal with 7 seconds remaining in the game. Bedlam broke loose, we won our first game, actually the first of 31 we would win that season on the way to winning the first AISA championship.

Obviously, I must have learned something that season. My reason for writing this book is to ensure that present and future coaches of indoor teams do not have to learn the game the hard way like I did. This book is intended as a practical guide for the coach and player and as an aid for the spectator who is interested in learning more about the game.

Packed arenas for indoor soccer began in 1974.

HISTORY OF INDOOR SOCCER

Indoor soccer as it is played today began in the Philadelphia Spectrum during the winter of 1974 when the Philadelphia Atoms of the North American Soccer League hosted the Soviet Red Army team. Over 13.000 fans witnessed the historic "first". Among those in attendance were Earl Foreman and Ed Tepper, future founders of the first professional indoor soccer league in this country.

What made the 1974 game different was that it was played on artificial turf on a field enclosed with dasher boards. Indoor soccer had been played for years in many of our larger cities, notably in St Louis and Chicago. In St Louis the game was called Hoc-Soc, or Hockey-Soccer, a fitting name considering the sport in many ways is a hybrid of hockey and soccer, combining the most exciting elements of both sports. There was not a uniform set of rules, however, and dasher boards were nonexistent.

It was not until 1977, in the midst of the greatest popularity soccer has ever known in the U.S., that a professional indoor league came into existence. A dozen businessmen met in New York on November 10, 1977 and put together an indoor league, subsequently called the Major Indoor Soccer League (MISL). Six charter franchises were awarded for the 1977-1978 inaugural season in Cincinnati, Cleveland, New York, Houston, Pittsburgh and Philadelphia. The league later expanded to over a dozen franchises from coast to coast and cities like Cleveland, St Louis and Kansas City were averaging between 12,000 and 14,000 spectators per game.

The MISL was dominated by two clubs. In the early years of the league, the New York Arrows, led by the indomitable Steve Zungul, won the league championship every year between 1979 and 1982. Zungul then took his act to San Diego where he led the Sockers to championships in 1983, 1985 an 1986. The league ceased operations in 1989.

One spinoff of the MISL success was the formation of a regional league called the American Indoor Soccer Association (AISA). The AISA was formed in 1984 with 6 charter franchises in Canton, Columbus, Louisville, Chicago, Milwaukee and Kalamazoo. The Canton Invaders proved to be the class of the AISA by winning championships in 1985, 1986, 1988, 1989 and 1990.

In 1990 the AISA evolved into a national league called the National Professional Soccer League, with franchises from coast to coast including Canada and Mexico.

Another offshoot of professional indoor soccer has been the proliferation of indoor soccer facilities. Thousands of youngsters and adults, both men and women, are currently enrolled in indoor soccer programs across the country. Indoor soccer has become a year-round activity and the rapid growth of indoor soccer facilities further indicates the popularity of the game in the United States.

SPECTATOR GUIDE TO INDOOR SOCCER

At first glance, indoor soccer might appear as a helter-skelter, slam-bang affair. It will not be long, however, before you will find yourself caught up in the action and emotion of the game. The indoor game was created with the spectator in mind. It is fast-paced, intense and high-scoring, with teams averaging at least a shot on goal every minute. Where many outdoor games result in 1-0 scores, indoor scores of 10-8 or 8-6 are not uncommon. Professional games average up to ten goals per game or more.

The attraction of the indoor soccer is that it is easy to comprehend, even by fans who know little about the game. However, once spectators start familiarizing themselves with the rules and some of the basic tactics, they will start understanding the game to a greater degree and subsequently enjoy it more. They will find that in spite of the speed of the game, there are organized patterns of play.

I. THE FIELD

The game is played on a field 200 by 85 feet, although the dimensions may vary somewhat from arena to arena. Dasherboards, 3½ to 4 feet high, usually topped by plexiglass, surround the field. Players' benches are behind the dasher boards at midfield. The playing surface consists of artificial turf, similar to astroturf. The ball is a standard soccer ball. The goal is 6 feet 6 inches high and 12 feet wide and extends beyond the boards at both ends of the field.

The field is divided by three lines, a midfield line and two red lines. A red line violation occurs when a forward pass crosses both red lines in the air without being touched by another player. For this violation, a change of possession and an indirect free kick from the red line restarts play.

Quick movement with the ball is the result of superior skill and conditioning.

II. THE TEAM

The game is played six aside, including the goalkeeper. The names given to the traditional positions on the field are defenders, midfielders, forwards, and a goalkeeper. All teams play with 2 defenders, 1 or 2 midfielders and 1 or 2 forwards.

GOALKEEPER - The goalkeeper is the only player on the field allowed to handle the ball, provided he does so within his penalty box. Outside the penalty box he is like any other player. The goalkeeper's priority is to make saves, preventing the ball from going into the goal. He may face up to 50 shots on goal, often from close range with speeds of up to 80 miles per hour. It is no wonder, therefore, that the goalkeeper's position is considered the most important to the team.

Another dimension of the indoor goalkeeper is the role in attack. The moment he gains possession of the ball he must start the attack either by throwing or passing the ball to a teammate or dribbling the ball out himself and passing it off to a teammate. Being able to play with the feet is a necessary skill for the indoor keeper. The GK of the future will be as proficient with his feet as he is with his hands.

DEFENDERS - The requirement of defenders is to defend, preventing opponents from scoring goals. They must be physically strong and quick, and have good tackling and shot blocking ability. In addition they must be disciplined man-to-man markers.

On attack defenders must be able to launch a counter attack or go on an overlapping run. An overlapping run is a forward run by a defender usually finishing with a shot on goal. When their teammates in front of them have the ball the defenders must take up good supporting positions so the ball can be played back to them.

MIDFIELDERS - Midfielders play a key role in indoor soccer. They must be all around players, physically very fit and able to attack and defend. The midfield player is generally the playmaker on the team, the quarterback. They act as links between the attack and defense. They must have high work rates, for often they find themselves in their own goal area and the next moment in front of the opponent's goal. On attack they must be good distributors of the ball, provide support for their forward players and have the ability to score goals.

On defense the midfield player must delay the opposition from attacking by denying them a chance to set up plays. He may also be forced to challenge an opposing defender with the ball, one who has beaten a forward.

FORWARDS - It is the job of the forwards to score goals.

However, they must also be able to switch from attack to defense the moment ball possession is lost. There are basically two kinds of forwards. If a team employs two forwards, they must be quick and mobile. Through interchanging of positions and running into open space they try to rid themselves of defenders marking them in order to get free for a shot on goal or receive a pass from a teammate. They must also have good dribbling ability and have the confidence to directly take on opponents, one on one. Having a nose for the goal and having the anticipation to play balls coming off the boards are invaluable assets for forwards.

Sometimes teams play with only one forward, called a **target player**. A target player must have the ability to play with his back to the goal. He must be physically strong and have the ability to hold and shield the ball until support arrives. When balls are played into him, he can play them off to a teammate, execute a one-two pass or turn and shoot. Although he has defensive responsibilities when ball possession is lost, the target player is primarily an attacking player whose main function is to provide a long target for his teammates.

FORMATIONS - The individual characteristics of the players will determine what kind of formation a team employs. A team needs at least a goalkeeper, two defenders, one midfielder and one forward. That leaves two players left to assign, and it is what we do with these 2 players that will determine the system. The two basic systems therefore are 2-2-1 (2 midfielders and 1 forward) or 2-1-2 (1 midfielder and 2 forwards). It must be remembered that systems don't win games, players do. No system will make up for bad passing and poor shooting. A system is basically a framework around which the team functions. All players have roles to play within each system, a plan which may change from game to game.

III. THE GAME

The game consists of four 15-minute quarters. There is free and unlimited substitution, as in hockey. Players may change "on the fly" during the game by jumping over the boards or going through the gate. When the ball is out of play, time is held up for 30 seconds. This enables coaches to send a new line on the field.

A unit of 5 players is called a **Line**. Generally the same 5 players will play on the same line. Indoor teams generally play with two set lines, with the additional players used as substitutes or used on specialty teams. **Specialty teams** are specialized units of players who take the floor when a team has a Power Play or is playing a man or more short.

A line in pro soccer is generally on the field for a total of 2 minutes. This is called a **Shift**. After a 2 minute shift the next Line comes in and this is called a **Line Change**.

An intriguing aspect of the indoor game are time penalties. Players who commit flagrant violations will be assessed a 2 minute penalty. The wrongdoer must spend 2 minutes in the penalty box, sometimes referred to as the "Sin Bin", during which time his team plays a man short. This results in the other team having a **Power Play**, where for 2 minutes the team has a numerical advantage of 5 vs 4 until a goal has been scored or time has elapsed. Goals are often scored during this period.

Indoor soccer, much like basketball or hockey, is a transition game. Teams who can convert quickly from defense to attack and vice-versa will have a significant advantage over a slower team.

Look for teams to play either High Pressure or Low Pressure when they lose possession of the ball. **High Pressure** is the equivalent of a full court press in basketball, with the team attempting to regain possession in the opponent's half.

Teams that elect to play **Low Pressure** will drop back to the half way line or their own red line and organize their defense from that point.

On attack, look for counter-attacks. A **Counter-attack** occurs when a team wins possession of the ball in its own half and quickly breaks out on attack, hoping to create a numerical advantage in the opponent's half. If a team plays with a **Target player** (a single forward), the first or second pass upon gaining possession will usually be played to him.

Now that you know what to look for, sit back, relax and enjoy the game.

Skills demand flexibility. A high pass is received with the inside of the foot.

INDOOR PLAYING SKILLS

T o be effective indoors, players must have the ability to control a ball under pressure almost instantly. Because of the confined area, time and space are at a premium and players are forced to make decisions quickly.

In order to become an effective indoor player, players must learn to perform all skills at top speed. Indoor soccer does not provide players the luxury of receiving the ball unopposed and being allowed time to make decisions. The pace of the game demands almost instant decision-making. Players who cannot perform basic skills at top speed will be at a significant disadvantage. Lack of skill results in loss of possession and a team obviously cannot score if it does not have the ball.

The dribbling, passing and shooting skills are the primary tools of the indoor player. A closer examination of each skill will reveal how these skills can be used most effectively indoors.

DRIBBLING

When for a variety of reasons a player cannot pass the ball to a teammate, it is necessary to control the ball by dribbling. Players who have the ability to beat another player one-on-one are invaluable indoors. There are no extra defenders like a sweeper in indoor soccer. Forwards, therefore, have many opportunities to take on a defender. Good dribblers should be encouraged to take on defenders in the attacking-third of the field. Dribbling is one of the most exciting elements of the indoor game.

Dribbling is very much an individual thing. Every player will sooner or later discover his own individual dribbling style. Through repetition of various dribbling moves players learn composure under pressure. They must develop the confidence to take opponents on, hold and shield the ball under pressure, and improvise. Too many players panic when confronted by one or more opponents. The ability to shield the ball (placing the body sideways between the ball and the opponent) is of particular importance in indoor soccer. In outdoor soccer a player often has time to receive a ball and turn. In indoor soccer a player generally finds himself under pressure of an opponent the moment the ball is played to him.

Dribbling is a combination of guiding the ball, driving the ball, stopping, turning, changing direction, changing of pace and using feints. There are three basic requirements for an effective dribbling technique:

1. Players must keep the ball within playing distance, no matter how fast they are running. This is particularly true indoors, where space is limited and players have less time to control the ball.

2. Players must keep their eyes up by looking over the ball so they can see the field of action around them and be able to change speed and direction instantly. Players who look at the ball while they are dribbling will not be able to see their teammates or the opponents.

3. When dribbling under pressure, screen the ball from the opponent by keeping your body between the ball and the opponent.

TACTICAL GUIDELINES FOR DRIBBLING:

1. Taking an opponent on one-on-one should occur in the attacking one-third of the field. Do not take opponents on in your own half of the field since loss of possession there could result in a goal for the opposition.

2. A pass is faster than the quickest player with the ball. Dribbling is discouraged when it is possible to pass to a teammate in a better position.

3. When there is no opportunity to make a pass, a player must dribble, thus keeping possession.

4. Do not dribble toward a teammate unless it is intended he should take over the ball, or he is to provide a target for a wallpass.

5. Do not begin to dribble from a standing position. Try to receive the ball on the run and start feinting movements while on the run.

6. Do not take on an opponent one on one if there is a covering player behind the challenging player. Even if you are successful in beating the first player the second player will obviously intercept the ball. When confronted by 2 opponents,

the obvious decision is to pass to the open teammate.

Feinting movements form the basis of a good dribbling technique. Feinting entails disguise and deception. The player with the ball attempts to deceive his opponent into thinking he is going in one direction. A good feint will result in a defender committing himself prematurely, at which time the player with the ball will take the ball the other way and sprint by him.

There are an immense number of dribbling variations and feinting moves. It is not within the scope of this book to deal separately with all of the various dribbling techniques. The exercises listed here lend themselves well to indoor training. An effective method of teaching dribbling involves 5 basic steps.

1. BASIC TECHNIQUES - Teaching players to control body and ball through multiple ball contacts.
2. Teaching players to keep possession under pressure of one or more opponents.
   a. ability to hold the ball
3. ADVANCED TECHNIQUES - Teaching players individual moves.
   a. Changing pace and direction
   b. Getting behind opponents
   c. Feinting movements
   d. Creating and improvisation
4. Teaching players to perform individual moves while under pressure of opponent.
   a. Token to passive opposition
   b. Active opposition
5. Teaching players to perform individual moves under game conditions

I BASIC TECHNIQUE EXERCISES
1. RESTRICTED AREA - Every player has one ball. Normal dribbling by all players - try not to run into other players.
   a. Alternately touch ball with inside of left foot, then inside of right foot.
   b. Dribble only with inside and outside of same foot.
   c. Dribble alternately outside of right foot and outside of left foot.
   d. Instruct players to sprint into an open space when they see one.
   e. Play tag in threes - tag one of two partners while keeping possession of own ball.
2. Sole of foot exercises
   a. Stroke ball sideways with sole of one foot and stop with inside

Under pressure from two opponents.

of other foot.

b. Pull ball back with sole of foot, stop with inside of same foot and dribble out to side with inside of other foot.

c. Pull ball back with sole of foot and go in opposite direction with outside of other foot. Turn body to side of ball.

d. Pull ball back with sole of foot, pivot and dribble ball out to side with inside or outside of same foot.

e. Stop-Feint - Player stops suddenly by pulling ball back with sole of foot and immediately dribbling forward again with inside or outside of same foot.

f. Pull ball back with select foot behind standing leg and take ball to side with inside of same foot.

g. Pull ball across body with one foot and go forward with inside of other foot.

h. Pull ball across body with one foot and dribble out to side with outside of other foot.

i. Step on ball with one foot, step past ball and come back with outside of other foot.

II. KEEPING POSSESSION UNDER PRESSURE OF ONE OR MORE OPPONENTS

1. 1 v 1 - Players divided up in pairs in restricted areas. Player in possession must screen ball from his partner. If partner gains possession, players change roles.

2. 1 v 2 - Three players, one ball. Player in possession attempts to screen ball from other 2 players.

III. ADVANCED TECHNIQUES

1. Cut ball with inside of instep in front of body and dribble out to side with outside of other foot.

2. Cut ball with inside of instep underneath body and dribble back with inside of other foot.

3. Cut ball with inside of instep and dribble back with outside of same foot.

4. Dribble ball to left with inside of foot and then immediately dribble right with outside of same foot.

5. Spin turns:

a. Bring outside of foot around ball, pivot and proceed in opposite direction with outside of same foot.

b. Same as above but proceed with inside of opposite foot.

6. Feint kicks:

a. Feint kick. At last moment take ball to side with outside of kicking foot.

b. Feint kick. At last moment take ball behind standing leg and dribble out to side.

c. Feint kick. At last moment pull ball back and go in opposite direction.

d. Feint kick next to ball and dribble forward with same foot.

7. Fake back heel - Bring one foot over ball and back and proceed to dribble in same direction.

8. Scissors - Bring one foot around inside of ball and dribble in other direction with outside instep of other foot.

IV. PERFORMING INDIVIDUAL MOVES UNDER PRESSURE OF OPPONENT

1. In fours - Small goal in middle. 2 players on one side of goal go 1 v 1 until shot has been taken. Players on other side then go 1 v 1. Players rotate being goalkeepers.

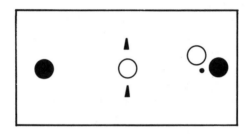

DIAGRAM 1

2. In sixes (same format as No. 1) - 1 v 2. Player in possession must attempt to beat other 2 players and finish with shot on goal. Players rotate being goalkeepers.

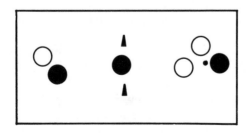

DIAGRAM 2

O = Defender
● = Attacker

3. In fours - Players on outside are stationed as goals. Goal is scored when ball passed between goalkeepers legs. Rotate after 1 minute.

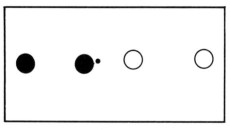

DIAGRAM 3

4. 1 + 1 v 1 - Server serves ball to teammate who must attempt to beat defender and score. Players change roles when possession changes.

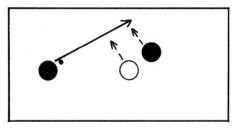

DIAGRAM 4

5. 1 v 1 with 2 neutral players - Players on outside can be utilized for one-two passes (with or without goalkeepers).

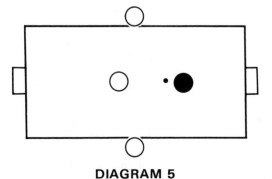

DIAGRAM 5

O = Defender
● = Attacker

6. Several other 1 v 1 drills are discussed under section dealing with **shooting**.

V. PERFORMING INDIVIDUAL MOVES UNDER GAME CONDITIONS

1. 5 v 5 to 10 v 10
   a. To two goals.
   b. Restrictions:
      1) Player must perform individual move before passing ball.
      2) Passive opposition by defenders - no tackling.
      3) Defenders provide active opposition.

PASSING

As with basketball and hockey, passing is the foundation of the game of soccer. It is no exaggeration to state that if a team cannot pass the ball proficiently, they cannot play the game. A team cannot score unless it has the ball and the longer it is able to maintain possession, the better the scoring chances.

Basically, passing is the skill of propelling the ball with either foot to a teammate in such a way that the receiving player can usually take the ball into his stride without slowing down. Passes may be made with the following parts of the body: inside and outside of foot, instep, heel and toe. The game will dictate which part of the foot is the most effective in a given situation.

In indoor soccer the most common pass is with the inside of the foot, commonly called the **push pass**. The inside of the foot pass is the most accurate and should be used for short distances (10 - 15 yards). For longer distances the instep should be used.

The **outside of the foot pass** has the advantage of not telegraphing the direction of the pass.

The **chip pass** or **lob pass** is a high pass over the heads of the defenders to a teammate positioned behind the defenders or running on to the ball.

A **toe pass**, although not as accurate, can be effective when the ball is almost out of a player's reach.

A **heel pass** is utilized when a player wants to play the ball backwards to a teammate.

A **thru pass** or **penetrating pass** (sometimes referred to as a "Killer Pass") involves kicking the ball between or over the defenders to a teammate who is in a good position to shoot on goal.

Combination passes are short, low passes between two or more players with the emphasis of keeping possession of the ball in order to move toward the opponent's goal. This often results in a shot on goal.

A **wall pass** is similar to the "give and go" in basketball, whereby a player challenged by an opponent makes a short pass to a nearby teammate. He then sprints into open space around the defender to receive the return pass. A wall pass is also a pass against the boards to a teammate or passing the ball against the boards and collecting the rebound yourself.

Because players play in a confined area it is important to pass to teammates' feet. If a pass is made to a player on the run it should be passed just in front of the receiving player. Thusly, he can take the ball into stride without slowing down or stopping.

Passing exercises should always begin with players moving about, passing on the run and receiving on the run. It is a serious error for players to stop every time the ball is played to them. They must learn to look for teammates as they are moving with the ball. Stationary drills, even at the beginner level, should be eliminated from all training sessions. Training must be match-related, and all exercises should reflect the game itself. Passing exercises should use the following format, based on progression:

1. Passing and moving.
2. Passing and moving at speed.
3. Passing with attacking team having numerical superiority.
4. Passing with equal number of attackers and defenders.
5. Passing with defenders having numerical superiority.
6. Technical/Tactical training.

PASSING EXERCISES
Warm-up Routine
1. Players divided in pairs in restricted area.
   a. Jogging pace - groups intermingle, concentrate and look for quickest possible pass.
   b. Ball served to receiving player who takes ball to side and moves in different direction.
   c. Receiver makes sprint into open space, at which time ball is passed to him.
   d. Takeovers - in front - player without ball runs to player with ball and takes ball from him.
   Note - player with ball must screen ball from potential defender and player without ball must make his run on side of ball.
   From behind, player without ball makes his run behind player with ball, who plays ball back to teammate by pulling ball backward with sole of foot.

   e. Alternate takeovers from behind and in front, followed by regular pass.
   f. One-two's - jogging pace. at appropriate time 2 players do a one-two pass between them.
      Variation: Alternately do a takeover and then a one-two pass.
2. Players divided up in threes in restricted area.
   a. Pass to teammate and follow the pass.
   b. Takeover between two players and regular pass to third player. Player with ball must hold ball until third player makes run into space.
   c. One-two pass between 2 players and regular pass to third player.
   d. One-two pass with pass going to third player. Player 1 passes to 2 and makes run for return pass. Instead 2 plays ball direct to player 3 (see diagram 1).

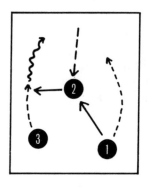

DIAGRAM 1

ALL SOCCER TRAINING MUST BE MATCH-RELATED.

e. Two balls - All players are moving. Player without ball shows for one-two passes.

f. Takeover between 2 players and one-two with third player.

g. One-two with one man on. Receiver marked by defender must run free of his man, show for ball and make return pass to teammate.

h. Long passing - A passes long to B. C makes support run and ball is played to C. C then passes long to A and B supports.

3. 5 v 2 in restricted area - 3, 2 or 1 touch.

4. 4 v 2 in restricted area - 3, 2 or 1 touch.

   a. 4 players. Concentrate on through passes.

   b. 2 players. Concentrate on challenging and covering and preventing through pass.

5. 4 + 1 v 2 in restricted area - 4 attackers on outside, 2 defenders and 1 attacking player in the middle. Attacker in middle must show for ball, hold, dribble, play direct, and one-two's. Players on outside have limited touches - 3, 2 or 1 touch.

6. Passing and mobility (see diagram 2)

   a. 3 v 1 - Two free players who serve balls to teammate. Player marked must continually show for ball through feinting movements and check runs.

   1) Defender stands behind receiver.

   2) Defender stands in front of receiver.

   b. Same as above but in groups of 6, with 2 players marked by defenders and 2 servers.

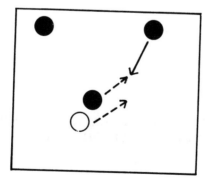

DIAGRAM 2

O = Defender
● = Attacker

7. Showing for the ball (see diagram 3)
   a. 5 players - one ball. Player 1 plays ball to Player 2, Player 3
      and Player 4.
      1) one touch passes by 2, 3, 4 and 5
      2) #1 can play 2 or 1 touch
      3) Rotate position of #1

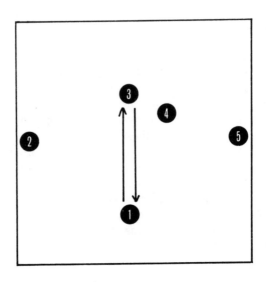

DIAGRAM 3

*THE ABILITY TO MAKE DECISIONS QUICKLY IS AN
ESSENTIAL PART OF THE INDOOR GAME.*

b. Same as a., but now players 2, 3, 4 and 5 must make checking runs - running away from ball, turning and meeting pass from Player 1 (see diagram 4).
   1) Add token or passive defender
   2) Add active defender.

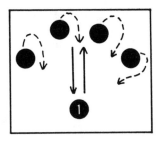

DIAGRAM 4

c. Same as a., but now players 2, 3, 4 and 5 run a few steps toward ball, check and turn and ball is played over their heads.
   1) Add token or passive defender
   2) Add active defender
   Defenders must be instructed to mark tight.

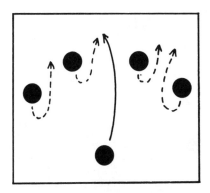

DIAGRAM 5

8. 2 v 2 in one half of field. Players are split up into groups of 4. players within each group go 2 v 2 for maximum of 3 minutes.
9. 5 v 5; 6 v 6; 7 v 7; 8 v 8; 9 v 9; 10 v 10 - one half of field or entire field.
   a. Possession - 5 or 10 passes equals 1 point.
   b. 3, 2 or 1 touch.
   c. Every successful one-two pass equals 1 point.
   d. Every successful takeover equals one point.
10. 5 v 5 to 10 v 10 with 1 neutral player.
    a. 3, 2 or 1 touch.
    b. Neutral player always on team that has possession and has unlimited touches.
11. Three teams of 6 players (see diagram 6)
    a. 6 v 6 over entire field with 6 players stationed outside touchline near boards.
    b. Players near boards can be utilized for one two passes - in effect team in possession has numerical advantage of 9 v 6.
    c. Rotate teams after 3 minutes.
    d. Restrictions:
       1) 3 or 2 touches per player
       2) Unlimited touches in attacking zone
       3) Players at boards allowed 2 touches or must play direct.
       4) Players stationed at boards are all neutral players.

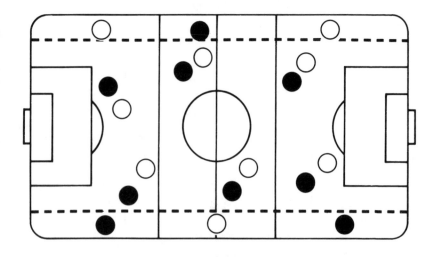

DIAGRAM 6

SHOOTING

Everything in soccer revolves around scoring and preventing opponents from doing the same. In indoor soccer the number of shots on goal range anywhere from 20 to 50 per team. The importance of shooting therefore can not be overemphasized. The challenge to the coach is to develop goal scorers, players who are composed under pressure. The coaching emphasis should be placed on timing, accuracy and power. Players must be exposed to situations where they can see goal scoring opportunities when they occur. They must also be aware of when to pass to a teammate who is in a better position to shoot.

Attacking players are usually under considerable pressure in a game. In training these pressures should be simulated as much as possible. By constantly practicing scoring attempts, players will develop the confidence they need to become effective goal scorers. There are numerous variations of shooting technique, such as inside of the foot, outside of the foot, inside and outside of the instep, full instep, the toe and the heel. The game will dictate which technique a player will utilize. Basically, there are 4 steps in teaching shooting:
1. Shooting without opposition.
2. Shooting at speed.
3. Passive to active opposition.
   a. Attacking team has numerical superiority.
   b. Equal number of attackers and defenders.
   c. Defending team has numerical superiority.
4. Shooting under game conditions.

Shots on goal should generally be a mixture of accuracy and power. Obviously the closer to the goal the more emphasis there should be on accuracy. Farther away from the goal, powerful shots will have a greater degree of success. Near the goal it is best to use the inside of the foot for accuracy.

Shots on goal which come as a surprise are always more dangerous. Players should avoid a big windup by bringing their kicking leg back too far. A quick snap of the lower leg or a toe shot is much more effective. Players who use a big windup will find a good number of their shots blocked by an opponent.

Another element of surprise is to convert a pass directly without stopping the ball. Stopping the ball in order to bring it under control simply provides the opposition with more time to challenge you.

It is important for the attacking player to consider the position and movements of the goalkeeper. If the goalkeeper is covering the near corner of the goal during an attack from the side, the attacker's best chance is a shot into the far corner or a pass to a player at the far post.

When shooting on goal, always shoot low unless the goalkeeper is on the ground after attempting to make a save.

If the goalkeeper is coming out of his goal in a one on one situation, shoot while the goalkeeper is still moving forward. The goalkeeper will find it difficult to change direction while he is still moving forward.

Diagram 1 - Players in center circle. Dribble in and shoot on goal outside of penalty box. Players inside penalty box look for rebounds.

Diagram 2 - Players in center circle. Ball played on ground to target player at top of semi circle who gives a one-two pass to original player who shoots on goal.
Variations:
a. Ball played in air to target player who must control ball and pass ball off to teammate.
b. Ball played on ground or in air to target player who must control ball, turn and shoot on goal.
Note - After shot on goal player giving pass rotates with target player.

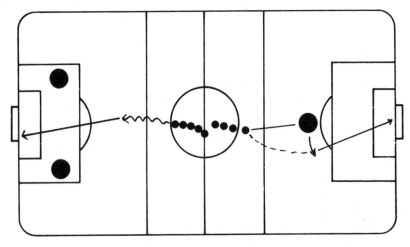

DIAGRAM 1   **DIAGRAM 2**

Diagram 3 - Two lines of players facing each other, about 8 yards apart. Front players of each line run at each other, one with ball and one without. When next to each other, players do a takeover, whereby player without ball takes ball from other player and shoots on goal.

Note - Player with ball must be goalside screening ball.

a. Fake takeover - Player with ball keeps ball and shoots.

Diagram 4 - Two lines of players outside of penalty box. Player with ball passes square to front player in other line and makes diagonal run for return pass and shoots on goal.

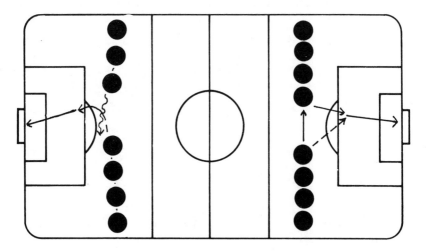

DIAGRAM 3   **DIAGRAM 4**

Diagram 5 - Ball played in to forward player who is marked by defender. Forward must turn and shoot. Begin with token opposition. Work from different angles.

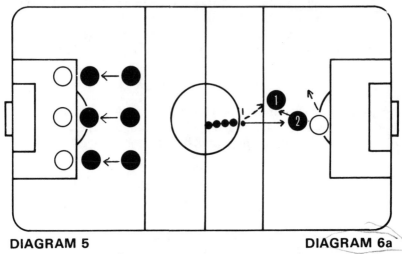

DIAGRAM 5   **DIAGRAM 6a**

Diagram 6 - Player 1 passes to Player 2 who is marked by defender.

a. Player 1 passes ball forward and creates 2 v 1 situation

b. Add extra attacker and defender and create 2 v 2 situation or 3 v 2 situation

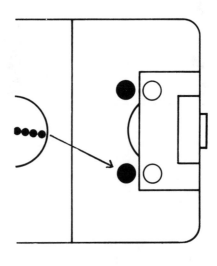

DIAGRAM 6b

Diagram 7 - Two lines of players. Player with ball makes forward pass to player without ball, who takes near post shot aiming for boards next to goal. Original player times run so he can kick rebound into goal.

Diagram 8 - Three lines of players. Player 1 makes lead pass to Player 2 who shoots far post to Player 3 who shoots on goal. Players rotate lines after each shot.

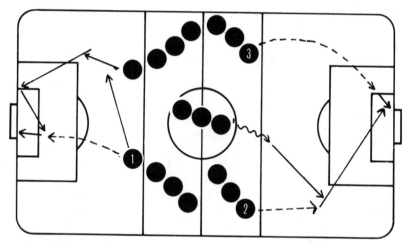

DIAGRAM 7   **DIAGRAM 8**

MOST GOALS ARE SCORED AT THE FAR POST. PLAYERS SHOULD BE ENCOURAGED TO SHOOT ACROSS THE GOALMOUTH.

Diagram 9 - Attacking players in center circle. Defending players on side near boards. Attacking player plays ball into defender who plays ball back first time to attacking player who must beat defender and shoot on goal. Players change roles after each turn.

Diagram 10 - A or B serve balls to Player 1 and Player 2. As soon as ball is served defender can become active. Player with ball has option to shoot first time or pass to teammate.

a. A and B should vary services, with different heights and velocities.

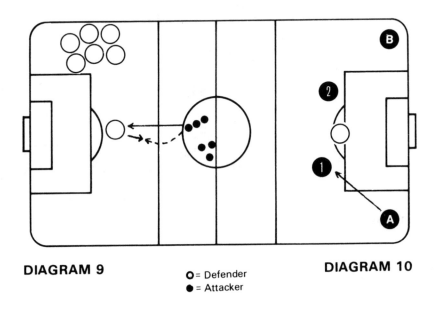

DIAGRAM 9

O = Defender
● = Attacker

DIAGRAM 10

COMPOSURE UNDER PRESSURE IS THE ULTIMATE AIM OF SOCCER TRAINING.

Diagram 11 - 3 v 3. Player with ball in center circle, defender 5 yards behind. At signal Player 1 sprints to goal and has option of shooting on goal or passing to Player 2 or Player 3. All three defenders become active the instant signal is given. If ball is passed to Player 2 or Player 3, they must attempt to shoot first time.

Diagram 12 - Four neutral players with ball, each in corner of square. Attacking player must vocally demand ball from 1 of 4 players, beat defender and shoot on goal. After each shot players change roles. Emphasis must be on getting free and finishing with speed.

a. At first no opposition, then token opposition, finally active opposition.

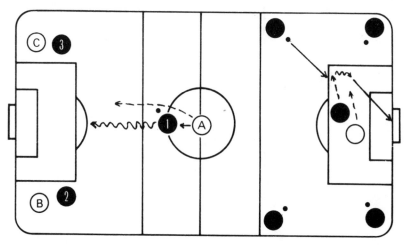

DIAGRAM 11   **DIAGRAM 12**

INDOOR PLAYERS MUST HAVE THE ABILITY TO BOTH ATTACK AND DEFEND.

O = Defender
● = Attacker

Diagram 13 - Player 1 passes to Player 2 who attempts to score. Moment pass is given two defenders become active and try to prevent Player 1 from scoring.

Diagram 14 - 2 v 1. Left forward dribbles toward goal. Once past cones he can shoot on goal or make far post pass to Player 2 who shoots on goal. Defender attempts to stop forward from scoring.

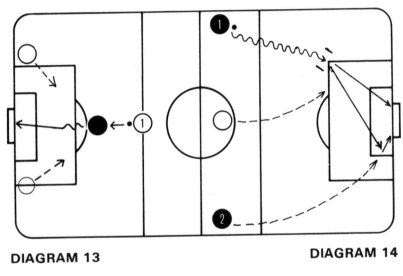

DIAGRAM 13   **DIAGRAM 14**

O = Defender
● = Attacker

ALL SOCCER TRAINING MUST HAVE THE BALL AS THE FOCAL POINT OF ACTIVITY.

Diagram 15 - 3 v 3. Forwards on outside have defenders behind them. Center forward has defender in front of him. At signal player with ball dribbles toward goal at which time defenders become active.

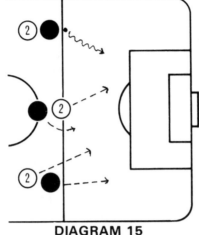

DIAGRAM 15

Diagram 16 - Player 1 passes to Player 2 who must show for ball and is marked by defender. Player 2 makes one-two pass to Player 1 and then spins around and looks for near or far postball from Player 1.

Diagram 17 - 2 v 1 in center circle. 3 v 3 in defensive zone. Attacking players must get free from marking and finish with shot on goal.

a. Player giving initial pass can become support player and create 4 v 3 situation.

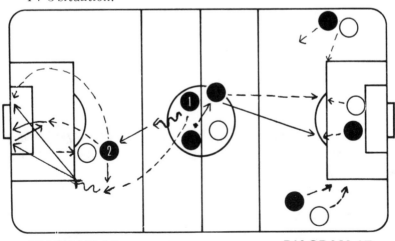

DIAGRAM 16   **DIAGRAM 17**

Diagram 18 - 6 v 6 in one half of field with 2 goals with emphasis on shooting.

Restrictions:

a. Every 3rd pass results in a shot.

b. Play three, two or one touch.

c. Can only shoot after successful take over.

d. Can only shoot after a successful one-two pass.

e. Emphasize near post or far post shots.

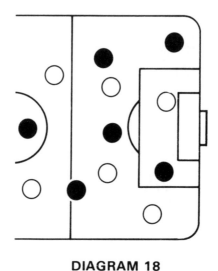

DIAGRAM 18

ALL PLAYERS MUST LEARN TO BE COMPOSED UNDER PRESSURE.

TECHNICAL/TACTICAL EXERCISES

Technical/Tactical training consists of exercises aimed at improving players' abilities to read the game and to make quick decisions. By simulating actual game conditions, players learn to recognize situations, to anticipate and to make the correct decisions. Players must know when to pass, dribble, shoot, when to make a run, and when to show (ask) for the ball. Through continual repetition of these exercises, players become aware of different options open to them and their decisions will become automatic when confronted with similar situations in a game.

Although these exercises are designed to improve the technical and tactical abilities of a player, there is a considerable amount of running involved so that the players' physical condition is simultaneously improved.

Diagram 1 - Possession game 3 v 1 in one half followed with pass to target player and finishing with shot on goal.
Options:

1) After receiving ball target player passes to one of two attacking players who finish with shot on goal.
2) Attackers must first interpass five times before passing to target player.
3) Restrict attackers to two touches of the ball.

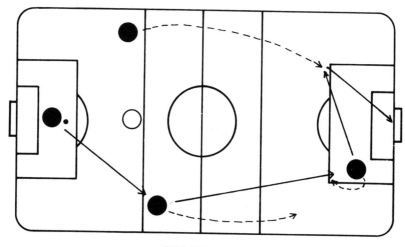

DIAGRAM 1

○ = Defender
● = Attacker

Diagram 2 - Possession game, 3 v 1 in one half followed with pass to target player in other half. After pass is made to target player two players on flank support target player. Defender also moves back.

Options:

1) Attackers must first interpass five times before passing to target player.
2) Play with target player in each half - after 5 consecutive passes ball must be passed to target player in other half.
3) If defender wins ball he becomes an attacking player. Attacking player who last touched ball becomes defender.

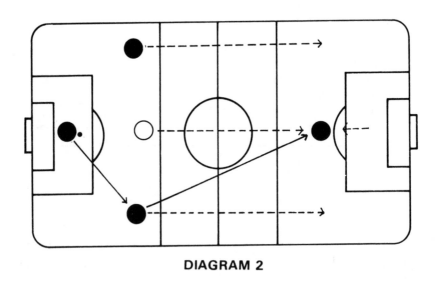

DIAGRAM 2

PASSING IS THE FOUNDATION OF SOCCER.

O = Defender
● = Attacker

Diagram 3 - Possession game 3 v 1 in own half followed with pass to target player who is marked by defender.

a. Two attacking players move up so 3 v 1 situation is again created in other half.

b. Two attackers and 1 defender can move into other half so 3 v 2 situation is created.

c. Three attackers and 1 defender can move into other half so 4 v 2 situation is created.

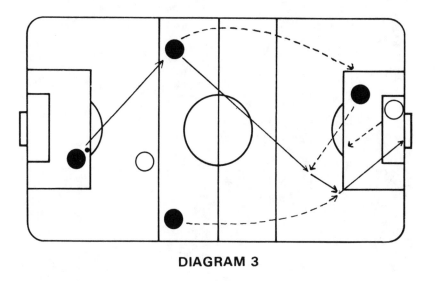

DIAGRAM 3

IMPROVISATION, THE ABILITY TO BEAT AN OPPONENT, MUST ALWAYS BE ENCOURAGED BY COACHES.

O = Defender
● = Attacker

The ability to look "beyond" the ball while keeping possession is an essential skill.

Diagram 4 - Possession game 3 v 2 in one half followed with pass to target player and finishing with shot on goal, or to far post.

a. Play 3 v 2 in own half followed with pass to target player, who passes to one of two supporting players who finish with shot on goal.

1) Attackers must interpass until target player shows for ball.
2) Restrict attackers to 3 or 2 touches of ball.

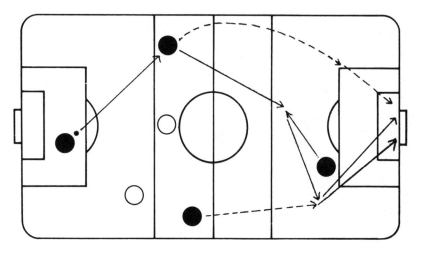

DIAGRAM 4

O = Defender
● = Attacker

CONCENTRATION AND DISCIPLINE ARE AT THE HEART OF A SUCCESSFUL TEAM.

Diagram 5 - Possession game 3 v 2 in one half followed by pass to target player, who is marked by a defender. Two attackers and one defender can move into other one half so that 3 v 2 situation is created.

Note - Target player may not score.

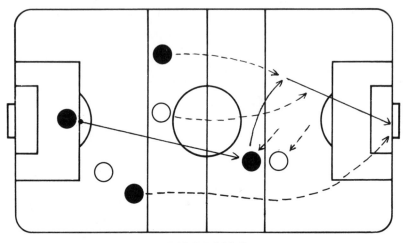

DIAGRAM 5

Diagram 6 - Possession game 3 v 2 in one half followed by pass to target player. Two attackers and two defenders can move into other one half, thereby creating a 3 v 2 situation. Player with ball may shoot or play ball to far post.

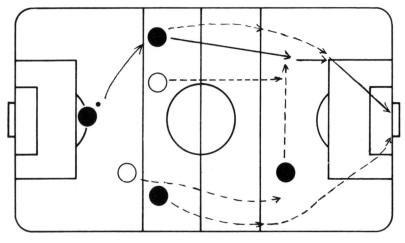

DIAGRAM 6

O = Defender
● = Attacker

Diagram 7 - Possession game 3 v 2 in one half followed by pass to target player. Three attackers and two defenders can move into other half thereby creating a 4 v 2 situation in other half. Player with ball can shoot or pass to far post.

Note - Target player must hold ball until support arrives.

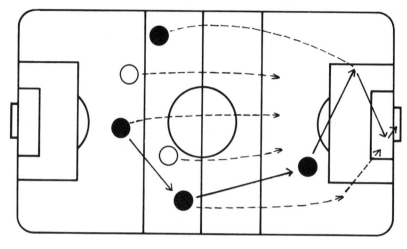

DIAGRAM 7

Diagram 8 - Possession game 3 v 2 in one half followed by pass to target player. Target player is marked by defender. Two attackers can move up thereby creating a 3 v 1 situation.

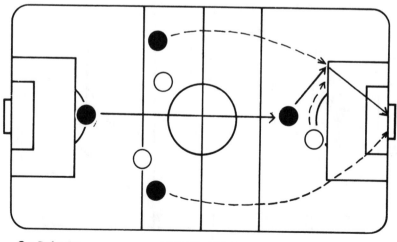

O = Defender
● = Attacker

DIAGRAM 8

Diagram 9 - Possession game 3 v 2 in one half followed by pass to target player. Target player marked by defender. Two attackers and one defender can move up, thereby creating 3 v 2 situation.

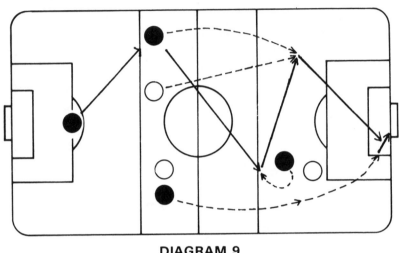

DIAGRAM 9

Diagram 10 - Possession game 3 v 2 in one half followed by pass to target player. Target player marked by defender. Two attackers and two defenders can go into other half thereby creating a 3 v 3 situation in attack.

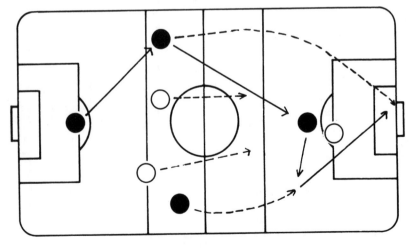

○ = Defender
● = Attacker

DIAGRAM 10

Diagram 11 - Possession game 3 v 2 in own half followed by pass to target player. Target player marked by defender. Three attackers and two defenders can move into other half creating 4 v 3 situation in attack.

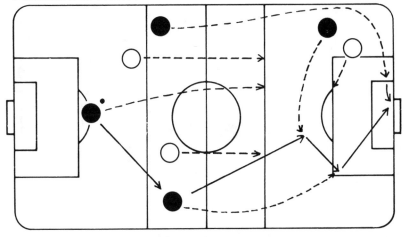

DIAGRAM 11

Diagram 12 - Possession game 3 v 3 in own half followed by pass to target player marked by defender. 2 Attackers and 2 defenders can move into other half thereby creating 3 v 5 situation in attack.

a. Target player must hold ball and then pass to one of two attacking players. He may not score himself.

  1) Target player is allowed to score.

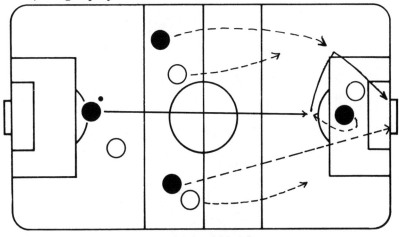

DIAGRAM 12

O = Defender
● = Attacker

-41-

TECHNICAL/TACTICAL EXERCISES - 5 v 5 Drills

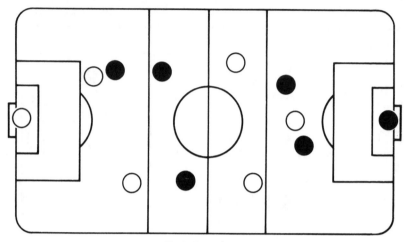

DIAGRAM 13

1. 3 V 2

3 attackers vs 2 defenders. Defenders and attackers must stay in own half. GK may throw ball short to defender or long to forward. When defenders have ball, forwards must apply pressure. When attackers have ball, defenders must delay them from getting shot off. Object of exercise is for defenders when they win ball to counter attack quickly by playing ball to one of three forwards. Forwards must show for the ball (see DIAGRAM 13a). At least 1 player should show short and another one long so player with ball has several options.

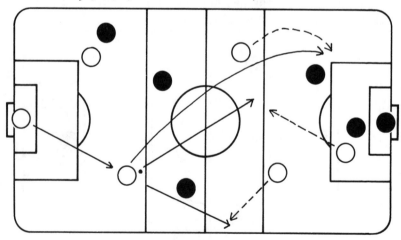

DIAGRAM 13a

● = Defender
○ = Attacker

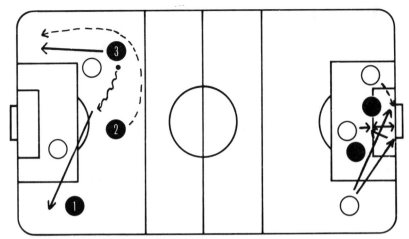

DIAGRAM 13b

Once ball is played in attacking half, it is important that player with ball always has two options.
In DIAGRAM 13b, player 2 runs around teammate 3 thereby giving player 2 two options. As a general rule, the player with the ball should have a player on either side of him.

DIAGRAM 13c

A 3 V 2 should finish with either a near post shot off the boards or a far post shot to a teammate running on to the ball.

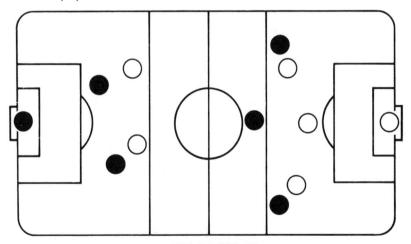

DIAGRAM 14

3 V 3 in one half and 2 V 2 in the other half.
Players must stay in their own half. GK should at times distribute short and at other times distribute long. Upon losing possession there must be a quick transition from attack to defense and vice versa.
Note: *Players must stay in their respective halves of the field.*

O = Defender
● = Attacker

TECHNICAL/TACTICAL EXERCISES

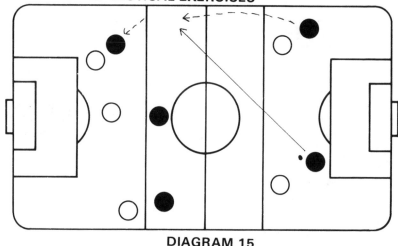

DIAGRAM 15

4 v 3 in one half and 2 v 1 in the other half.

a. Players start off 3 v 3 in one half and 2 v 2 in the other half (see DIAGRAM 14)

b. On attack, 1 player from the attacking team can cross the center line to create a numerical advantage for his team.

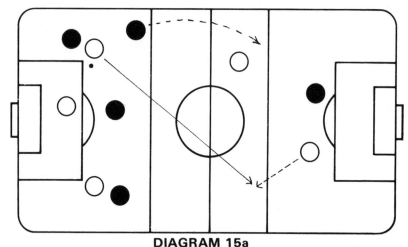

DIAGRAM 15a

c. 1 defender and 2 forwards must always stay back.

d. Once a 4 v 3 situation has been created in one half and ball possession is lost the team in possession must counter attack quickly to take advantage of the 2 v 1 situation in the other half (see DIAGRAM 15a).

e. the attacking player closest to his own half should sprint back in order to create a 2 v 2 situation (see DIAGRAM 15a).

TECHNICAL/TACTICAL EXERCISES

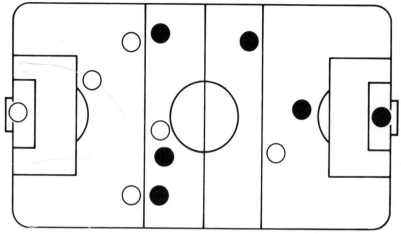

DIAGRAM 16

3 v 4 in one half and 1 v 2 in the other half. Defending team now has numerical advantage.

a. Teams start off 2 v 2 in one half and 3 v 3 in the other half.

O = Defender
● = Attacker

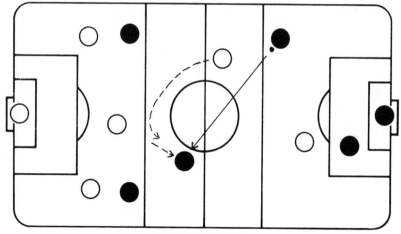

DIAGRAM 16a

b. Upon loss of possession, team can bring back all but 1 player. (see diagram 16a)
c. Defending team must always keep 2 players back in their own half.
Note: *Playing 3 v 4 the emphasis should be on keeping possession. As soon as possession has been won by 1 of 4 defenders first pass should go to target player in other half. Target player must hold ball until support has arrived.*

O = Defender
● = Attacker

Whether receiving or passing, the eyes should take in everything that's going on.

TECHNICAL/TACTICAL EXERCISES
Game of Keeping Possession

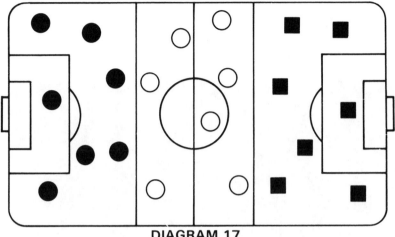

DIAGRAM 17

1. Game is started with 6 or 7 players in each zone.

a. A team in end section starts play with ball and they attempt to string together 5 consecutive passes.

b. Team adjacent to that team can send 3 players into their zone to try to break up string of passes.

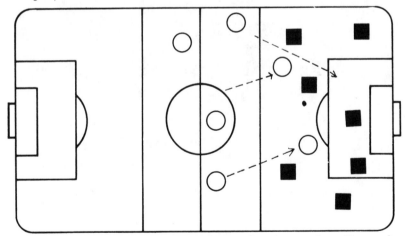

c. If 5 consecutive passes are made, ball is transferred to opposite end for a goal.

d. If defending team in middle breaks up 5 passes, they assume the new end spot and team that loses possession becomes the defenders in the center area.

e. Variations.
   1) Restrict players to 2 touches of the ball or 1 touch
   2) Adding more passes for a goal.

Good goalkeeping is at the heart of a successful team.

GOALKEEPING

There is numerous material dealing specifically with goalkeeping training. It is not within the scope of this book to go into a detailed discussion of goalkeeping techniques and tactics. This chapter will deal primarily with specific indoor techniques and tactics and is specifically directed toward the outdoor goalkeeper coming indoor and to the indoor keeper with limited experience.

Of all the positions, the goalkeeper position is probably the most altered when converting from outdoor soccer to indoor soccer. There are no high crosses to deal with, and there is no punting. In addition, there are the dasher boards to contend with. Instead of facing an average of perhaps 10 to 15 shots on goal, indoor keepers can expect up to 50 shots on goal, most at short range.

A team should carry two goalkeepers on their roster. On the professional level this is absolutely imperative. Playing up to fifty games in six months takes its toll in terms of injuries and lapses in concentration.

At the youth level it is also advisable to have two goalkeepers on the team. Friendly competiton usually brings out the best in players. Absenteism and injuries make it essential to have two goalkeepers. Goalkeeping training is often neglected because the coach either does not have the time to devote to it or he simply lacks knowledge about training of goalkeepers. The advantage of having two goalkeepers is that they can train each other. Goalkeeping is a specialized position and goalkeeper training must be an integral part of every practice. Since most teams do not have the luxury of a coach working with goalkeepers it is up to the players to conduct their own training.

Many goalkeeping exercises can be performed in twos with one keeper acting as a server.

EQUIPMENT - Goalkeepers will be falling on hard and abrasive surfaces and should wear long pants with padding as well as a long sleeve shirt with padding on the sleeves and elbows to protect themselves from rug burns and hard falls. Gloves are also a necessity.

From a safety standpoint, some kind of head gear might be beneficial since most goal areas are not padded.

PERSONAL QUALITIES

CONCENTRATION and COMPOSURE - The indoor game is an emotional game and a goalkeeper who allows his emotions to dominate his behavior in the goal will undoubtedly make errors in judgment and technique. The goalkeeper must be cool under pressure, and if he's scored upon his thoughts should not linger on what he should have done to prevent the goal. Instead, he must get ready for the next shot. Indoor keepers must get used to the fact that many more goals will be scored on them than outdoors.

CONFIDENCE - Anxiety produces pressure. The more the goalkeeper is exposed to game situations in practice the less anxious he will be when confronted with similar situations in the real game. An effective goalkeeper will exude confidence to his teammates. A goalkeeper who does not believe in his own ability wil be less than effective. Confidence comes with experience. How a goalkeeper reacts to adversity will to a large extent determine his effectiveness. A confident keeper will shrug off a bad game and get ready for the next one. A less confident keeper may still be thinking about the last game as he gets ready for the next one.

LEADERSHIP - As the last player in defense the goalkeeper must provide the leadership by continually directing, cajoling and encouraging his teammates in front of him.

COURAGE - Because of the confined playing surface there is a considerable amount of physical contact. A goalkeeper therefore must be aggressive and should dominate the area immediately in front of the goal. He must also show courage in stopping up to 50 shots a game, many coming from point blank range at speeds of up to 80 miles per hour. They are often forced to throw themselves in front of balls or dive at an attacker's feet. Only the brave will survive.

PHYSICAL QUALITIES

Since the indoor keeper rarely has to deal with high balls, being tall is not necessarily an advantage. What is important is **quickness**, **agility** and **flexibility**. The indoor keeper first and foremost must be a good athlete.

TECHNIQUE

The techniques of the goalkeeper can be divided into the following areas: throwing, positioning, catching high and low balls, diving, punching, deflections, dribbling and kicking.

Perfect technique is less important than the stopping of the ball. The indoor keeper must make saves with his feet, legs, body, arms, and hands. Because of the volume and rapidity of shots goalkeepers should be better shot blockers than shot catchers.

DEFLECTIONS - It is virtually impossible to catch hard shots at close range. Basically all a goalkeeper can do in these instances is to get a hand or foot on the ball and deflect it out of danger along the boards or over the top. Most saves a goalkeeper makes are basically deflections. "Safety First" should be the motto. Deciding when to catch a ball and when to deflect is probably the most important decision goalkeepers have to make. Experience will aid the keeper in determining when it is simply too dangerous to attempt to catch a ball.

When deflecting the ball it is not necessary to strike the ball with power. Guiding it with fingers or palm will do the job. When diving to the corners for low or medium high balls, the goalkeeper should use the bottom hand, which extends farther, to deflect the ball along the boards.

DISTRIBUTION - The goalkeeper is the first line of attack when he is in possession of the ball. Good distribution will ensure his team keeps possession. The keeper can bring the ball into play either by throwing the ball or by dribbling and passing. Punting is not useful because of the reduced playing area.

Throwing - A goalkeeper has 5 seconds to get rid of the ball. Good vision and a quick release are necessary in order to distribute the ball within 5 seconds. After making a save the keeper should strive to get to the top of the penalty box and distribute the ball from there. There are 2 basic kinds of throws.
1. Rolling ball along ground in underhand motion. An underhand throw is more accurate and should be used over distances not to exceed 30 yards.
2. Overhand throw should be used over longer distances. Care must be taken not to throw the ball across three lines. When throwing the ball long, the ball should be played either at the player's feet or in front of him to run on to.
Generally a goalkeeper should first look for a long target. The alternative is to roll the ball to a nearby teammate.

Dribbling and Passing - Dribbling and passing skills, rarely used outdoors, have become an essential part of the indoor keeper's repertoire. The keeper with limited ball control skills will find himself at a significant disadvantage. Keepers can be utilized to bring the ball out of the defense. This is a particularly useful tactic against teams that play a low pressure defense. By having the goalkeeper dribble the ball out of the defense, a numerical advantage is created.

POSITIONING

Goalkicks - Goalkeepers should take their own goalkicks. Allowing a defender to take a goalkick will mean one less player on the field.

1. If the ball is in the opposing half the goalkeeper should be at the top of the penalty box or outside it to intercept any through balls.
2. Goals should never be scored at the near post. Goalkeepers must cut off that option by covering the near post and the nearby board, thus forcing shots to the far post where the attacker's percentage of accuracy is reduced.
3. If an opponent has beaten the nearest defender, the keeper must come off his line to cut down the angle. If the opponent prepares to shoot, the keeper must stop, as his reactions will be better if he is standing still.
4. Goalkeepers should always be slightly off the line when an opponent is ready to shoot.
5. Balls coming off the boards immediately adjacent to the goal are a goalkeeper's nemesis. A goalkeeper must cover the near post when the opponent attacks from the side. When the ball is shot against the boards he must quickly readjust his position to either catch or deflect the ball as it comes off the boards or get back to the middle of the goal and get ready for the next shot.

RESTARTS

When the opponent has a free kick or corner kick, the goalkeeper should always have the ball in sight, ready to make a save. It is a mistake to tie up too many players in a defensive wall. A wall consisting of two players is sufficient.

Defending on free kicks and corner kicks should be rehearsed continually in practice, in order that each player knows his responsibility.

THE TRANSITION FROM ATTACK TO DEFENSE AND FROM DEFENSE TO ATTACK IS THE NAME OF THE GAME.

As soon as the save is made, the goalkeeper should look for the open player.

GOALKEEPING EXERCISES

Diagram 1 - Throwing. Two lines of players. Goalkeeper rolls ball along ground in underhand motion to front player in Line A, who takes ball into stride and passes to front player in Line B. Player in Line B dribbles toward goal and shoots.

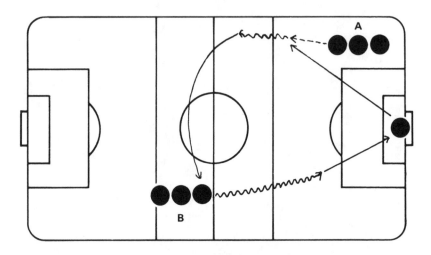

DIAGRAM 1.
Throwing - Underhand

There are times when the goalkeeper is under constant pressure from close-in.

Diagram 2 - Throwing. Two lines of players. Goalkeeper makes overhand throw to player in Line A who takes ball in his stride, dribbles towards goal and makes far post pass to player in Line B.

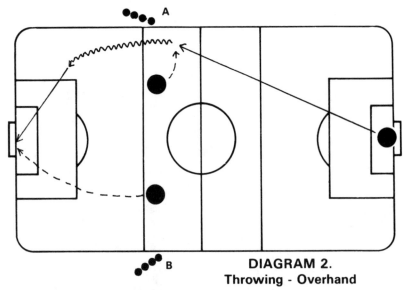

DIAGRAM 2.
Throwing - Overhand

Diagram 3 - Objective: Improvement of reaction time. Server lines up 8 to 10 soccer balls in semi circle and shoots them in rapid succession.
Note - After Goalkeeper makes save, wait until he is up before taking next shot.

Diagram 4 - Same as #3, but two players now alternately take shots, forcing Goalkeeper to adjust his position.

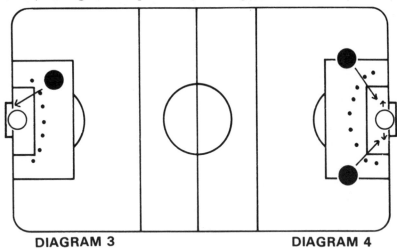

DIAGRAM 3   **DIAGRAM 4**

Sometimes the goalkeeper must venture outside of the penalty area.

Diagram 5 - Objective: Improvement of reaction time, courage, mental and physical toughness.
Two players line up approximately 6 yards from goal to outside of each goalpost, each with several soccer balls. Starting from middle, Goalkeeper adjusts his position to save a direct shot at goal from one player and then immediately runs across the goal to save a shot from other player.

Diagram 6 - Objective: Quick movement in the goal in dealing with high and low shots.
Server shoots a high ball to right of Goalkeeper. Keeper saves and rolls ball back to server who in meantime has shot a second ball low to the other corner which the Goalkeeper moves quickly to save.
a. Change sides, high and low.

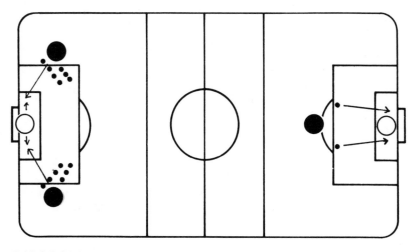

DIAGRAM 5   **DIAGRAM 6a**

IN GOALKEEPING, ONLY THE BRAVE SURVIVE.

Diagram 7 - Objective: Improvement of quick movement in the goal and agility (quick changes of direction).
Goalkeeper stands to side of goal and runs across goal to catch a ball out of the air served high; then turns around quickly to save a low ball tossed into the corner. Same from other side.

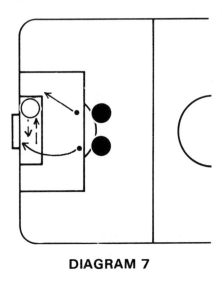

DIAGRAM 7

BY SETTING HIGH STANDARDS FOR THEMSELVES, COACHES WILL INFLUENCE PLAYERS TO DO THE SAME.

Diagram 8 - Objective: To intensify training for reaction time and for overall conditioning.

A. From center of field players dribble towards goal. Shots are taken from top of penalty box. Goalkeeper saves first shot and immediately gets ready for second. Third player looks for rebounds or can be third shooting player.

B. Balls are played forward to target players for one-two pass to passing player who shoots on goal. Goalkeeper must get up quickly for second and third shots and tempo must be kept fast.

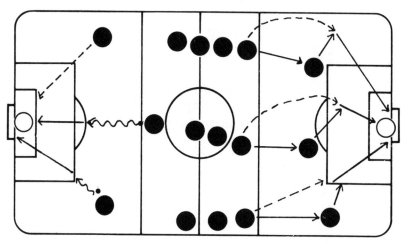

DIAGRAM 8a   **DIAGRAM 8b**

Diagram 9 - Objective: Sharpening reflexes.
Server shoots balls quickly at full strength to Goalkeeper's body or just to side of Goalkeeper with rapid repetition. Goalkeeper saves with feet, legs, body, arms or hands. Exercise can also be done with screening player obstructing Goalkeeper's vision. Server can shoot balls off floor or use drop kick.

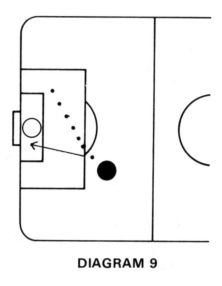

DIAGRAM 9

Diagram 10 - Objective: Improvement of quick movement in front of goal.

A. Player A serves low shot along ground to the post; Goalkeeper, dives to save ball and quickly returns ball to shooter A while at same time a ball is shot by player B low to opposite post.

B. On signal from coach Goalkeeper starts at center, runs over to touch goalpost and goes full length across goal to save a low ball delivered by server to opposite post. Goalkeeper then returns ball to server, resumes his position in middle of goal and waits for next signal.

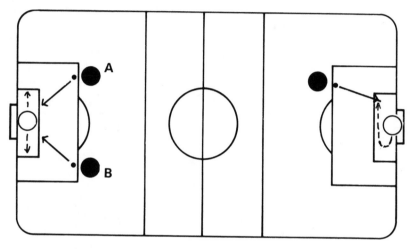

DIAGRAM 10a   **DIAGRAM 10b**

Diagram 11 - Objective: Saving far post balls. Player A drives ball to Player B at far post. GK starts at near post position and must quickly run and dive to other post and attempt to save shot from Player B.

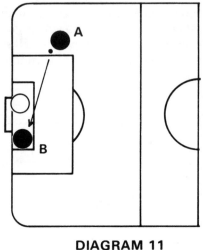

DIAGRAM 11

Diagram 12 - Objective: Saving near post balls.
Goalkeeper starts at center position and proceeds to cut off angle
at near post when Player A is ready to shoot. Goalkeeper must
attempt to save ball as it comes off the boards or get back to center
position to stop shot from Player B.
Note - If Goalkeeper is caught cheating by leaving near post
open, Player A should be instructed to shoot on goal.

Diagram 13 - Objective: Dealing with balls coming off glass.
Server shoots ball against glass at the curvature. GK must
attempt to save while opponent looks for rebounds.

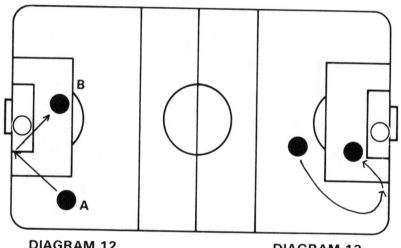

DIAGRAM 12   **DIAGRAM 13**

The defense must be organized. Here, three players take on two opponents.

PRINCIPLES
OF INDOOR SOCCER

The principles of soccer can be divided into Principles of Attack and Principles of Defense. In order for a team to fur ction as a cohesive unit, all coaches must understand these basic principles and players must be able to execute them. No matter what system of play a team employs, the principles of play remain the same.

The key moment in indoor soccer is how players react when ball possession changes. Similar to hockey and basketball, indoor soccer is a game of transition. One yardstick by which to measure the effectiveness of a team is the efficiency of its transition game. A team which is slow to react from attack to defense and back again will most likely find itself at a significant disadvantage and will be hard pressed to win.

The moment a team loses possession of the ball, all players think and play defense. Conversely, the moment a team gains possession all players must react instantly by beginning the transition to attack.

DEFENSE

The primary objective of defense is to prevent opponents from scoring. The secondary objective is to regain possession of the ball and initiate an attack.

Preventing opponents from scoring is best accomplished by denying opponents time and space in which to work. Discipline is at the heart of a good defense. Every player must know his role and the responsibilities which come with that role. An effective defense is no more or less than a united effort by a group of well disciplined players, all willing and able to back each other. Indoor soccer is a game of transition, when a team loses possession of the ball, all 5 players must make an immediate transformation from attack to defense.

Since the position of "sweeper" is foreign to indoor soccer, it is essential that each player contain his own immediate opponent. Defenders do not have the luxury of a free defender behind them, covering up for mistakes. More so than in outdoor soccer therefore, players have two basic responsibilities when defending: First, each player must mark his immediate opponent. Secondly, cover must be provided when a teammate is challenging for the ball.

Although some teams play strictly man to man defense, where each player is responsible for a specific opponent, others play a zone defense where each player covers a roughly defined zone. Generally the best method is a combination of the two. For example, most teams will play a zone defense in the middle and attacking third of the field but within their own defensive zone they will play strictly man to man.

There are two basic methods of defending when a team loses possession of the ball. One is called **HIGH PRESSURE**, the other one is called **LOW PRESSURE**. Which of these two methods a team uses is dictated first of all by its own personnel. Secondly, it may depend upon the playing style of the opponent.

HIGH PRESSURE

In indoor soccer, high pressure is the equivalent of forechecking in hockey. In basketball, it is called a full-court press. The aim of high pressure is to lock the opponent in his own half and make it difficult for him to get out. This is accomplished by attempting to regain possession of the ball at the place and moment possession is lost.

High pressure is particularly effective against teams whose players have difficulty passing under pressure. this is particularly true of defenders. Many defenders have a tendency to lose their composure when confronted or harassed by an opponent. On the other hand, if opposing defenders are quite skillful in bringing the ball out of the defense, high pressure may not be as effective. The basic principles of high pressure are:

1. Getting goalside of opponents the moment ball possession is lost.
2. The immediate chase by the player who lost the ball to the opponent.
3. Closing opponents down by placing them under immediate pressure, thus delaying opponent from attacking and giving time for teammates to get goalside of opponents and organize the defense. The player closest to opponent with ball must close him down.

4. When closing an opponent down, never face him head on. always approach at an angle so the opponent is forced to pass inside or outside. In the opponents half of the field it is preferable to force the play inside so the ball can be intercepted by another teammate. In your own half of the field the play should be forced to the outside.

   a. The two forwards should not be caught square when closing opponents down. Instead, they should be forcing the opposing defender to make a square pass. When one forward is challenging, the other forward must position himself so he can provide cover for his teammate and at the same time be able to close his opponent down should the ball be played square.

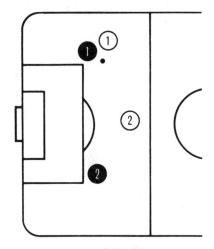

DIAGRAM I

Note - *Attacker Player 1 by positioning himself at an angle is forcing Defender Player 1 to pass inside. Player 2 is covering for Player 1. If ball is passed square to defending Player 2, Player 2 will immediately close him down and Player 1 covers Player 2.*

● = Defender
O = Attacker

5. If beaten, players must recover goalside of the ball and then look to pick up an opponent.
6. Control and Restraint. Players must exercise good judgment and discipline during transition from attack to

defense. Players must know when to win the ball (risky) or when to simply delay and contain. Jockeying is a skill all players must master. Overcommitting is a cardinal sin. Because there is no free defender every time a player overcommits, the opponent has a numerical superiority. It is good advice therefore to: a) stay on your feet; b) don't overcommit; c) keep your opponent in front of you. Remember, "Fools Rush In". Nowhere is this more true than in indoor soccer.

In order to high pressure effectively, it is important that the opposition be coaxed into bringing the ball up out of the defense. How can this be accomplished when the goalkeeper is in possession of the ball? First of all, the two forwards must drop back nearer to the opponents' red line. Except for the two opposing defenders, all other opponents must be marked man to man. The only outlet the goalkeeper has, therefore, are his two defenders. The moment the ball is played to one of the two defenders, one forward immediately closes him down, while the other forward provides cover.

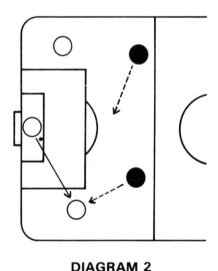

DIAGRAM 2

●= Defender
O= Attacker

If the defender in possession passes the ball back to the goalkeeper, the forward must chase the ball to the keeper, making sure he stays between the defender and the keeper. (Remember, the keeper may not handle the ball in this situation).

Obviously it is somewhat risky to chase the ball back to the keeper since one field player is now unmarked. To make it less risky, a midfield player can be instructed to position himself between the opponent he is marking and the opposing defender, in such a way that if the ball is played to either one he can immediately close him down.

An effective tactic is to mark one defender when the keeper has the ball and leave the other defender open. For example, if one defender has good skill and is good at building out of the defense, one forward should mark that defender, therefore encouraging the Goalkeeper to give the ball to the less skilled defender. Once he has the ball the other forward immediately closes him down. (see Diagram 3).

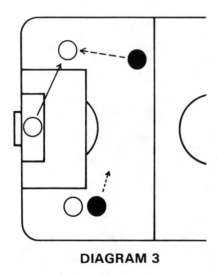

DIAGRAM 3

● = Defender
O = Attacker

An alternative to playing high pressure all over the field is to play high pressure in two-thirds of the field, starting at the opponent's red line. By organizing the defense from the red line, the field is made more compact, thus increasing the likelihood of intercepting a pass.

The equivalent of offside in indoor soccer is the Three Line Violation. A ball may not be played in the air from a team's defensive zone into the attacking zone, thus crossing three lines. All efforts should be directed towards winning the ball before it crosses the first red line.

When a team employs high pressure the Goalkeeper should position himself at the edge of the penalty box, acting as a last defender, anticipating any thru balls which might come his way.

The effectiveness of high pressure depends upon mobile and aggressive forwards. It must be a total team effort by all five players. If one player does not do his job, high pressure falls apart. Generally high pressure suits players who are very fit, have a high workrate and who possess a high degree of intensity and concentration.

Pressuring an opponent.

LOW PRESSURE

Low Pressure in indoor soccer is similar to a half-court press in basketball. Instead of attempting to regain possession of the ball in the opponent's half, the team which has lost possession withdraws into its own half before challenging for the ball. Low pressure is a particularly effective tactic against teams who rely on quick counter attacks when they gain possession. The aim of a counter-attack is to get behind defenders. By withdrawing quickly, an opponent is denied space into which the ball can be played. The basic principles of low pressure are:

1. All five players must get behind the **ball** upon losing possession.
2. Three players drop back immediately to their own red line. Two forwards must attempt to delay opponents from attacking by containing players with the ball.
   a. When ball possession is lost the player closest to the opponent who has won the ball must immediately close him down and delay the attack. (see dia. IV).

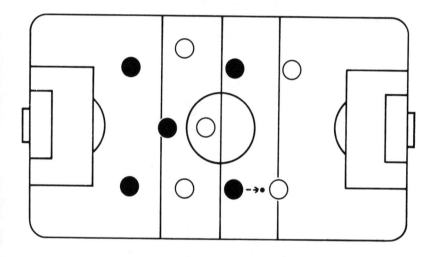

DIAGRAM IV

3. Once all five players have withdrawn well into their own half, all opponents must be marked man to man within the defensive third of the field. In other words, low pressure is in effect high pressure within the defensive zone.
   a. It is essential the two forwards keep the two opposing defenders in front of them.

4. Compactness is the key. When all five players withdraw into their defensive zone, the opponent is denied time and space.
5. Control and Restraint. As with high pressure, players must exercise good judgement and discipline. Keeping the opponent in front of you, not overcommitting, knowing when to tackle and when to retreat are only some of the decisions players have to make.
6. A very effective tactic is to **doubleteam** opponents when they are in possession of the ball near the boards. While he is being challenged in front by a defender, one of the forwards drops back and challenges the player from behind or from the side (see dia 2). This tactic is equally effective if a team plays high pressure (see dia V).

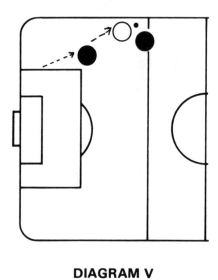

DIAGRAM V

SYSTEMS DO NOT WIN GAMES. PLAYERS DO.

O = Defender
● = Attacker

7. Upon winning possession, the team must counterattack quickly and attempt to get behind opposing defenders.

There are basically two variations of a low pressure defense. The most common is the half field defense whereby all 5 players withdraw into their own half of the field with the forwards representing the first line of defense at the halfway line.

A more conservative form of low pressure is for all 5 players to drop back within their own defensive zone thus in effect conceding two thirds of the field to their opponent. Under this system the defense is organized at the defending red line.

A low pressure defense is particularly suitable for a team with an effective counterattack. By withdrawing into its own half a team encourages the opposition to push their defenders up to the halfway line or beyond, leaving vital space behind them which can be exploited with a quick counterattack.

If a team does not possess forwards capable of winning the ball in the opponents half, a low pressure defense may be more suitable. Of course it is always possible to play high pressure with one line and low pressure with another. The system, simply, must suit the players.

PRINCIPLES OF ATTACK

There are two forms of attack in indoor soccer. One is a counter attack or breakaway. The other is a planned attack based upon a deliberate build-up out of the defense with the emphasis on possession. Which system a team elects to use is dictated by two factors:

1. Playing ability and tactical awareness of own players.
2. Playing style of opponent.

I COUNTER-ATTACK

A quick counter-attack may be likened to the "fast-break" in basketball. When a team has gained possession of the ball there must be an immediate transition to attack. The primary aim of the counter-attack is to get behind opponents with one or two passes and to finish with a shot on goal. A team is most vulnerable to a counter-attack when its attack breaks down in the attacking third of the field and it has committed many players into the attack. By a quick counter-attack the opposition seeks to establish a numerical superiority (2v1; 3v2; 4v3), hopefully resulting in a shot on goal.

The key ingredients for a successful counter-attack are:
1. If a team plays with a target player up front, that player must provide a target by showing for the ball (running into open space) at the right time. The right time is when the player in possession is ready to pass the ball. If a team plays with 2 forwards, they must break out quickly by running into open space and providing targets for the player with the ball. (see dia VI)

DIAGRAM VI

O = Defender
● = Attacker

2. Upon gaining possession the first or second pass should be played to the target player(s). Obviously dribbling the ball out of the defense will only give the opposition time to organize its defense.
3. The player (including the goalkeeper) who has gained possession of the ball in the defensive zone should always first look for a long target. Generally when a player is in possession of the ball, he needs players near him for short

support but also one or two players farther away from him for long support. Looking up for a long target first accomplishes two things:

a. If the target player is open the ball can be played to him directly.

b. By looking up the player uses his peripheral and penetrating vision so he can immediately see what is to the side and directly in front of him. If the long pass is not "on" therefore, he can pass the ball short to another teammate.

4. The target player must have the ability to hold the ball under pressure. If he finds himself 1v1 with an opponent he can either turn and take the opponent on, or hold the ball and wait for support and perhaps create a 2 v 1 situation. Any time he is confronted with two opponents he has no choice but to hold the ball until support arrives.

5. Once the ball has been played to a forward player, immediate support is needed. If support is not forthcoming immediately any numerical advantage the attacking team had will be lost. Time is always in favor of the defense.

A counter-attack is effective against teams who are slow getting behind the ball to mark opponents. It is also effective against teams who commit too many players into the attack and thus leave themselves shorthanded in the back. A team which relies on high pressure also may be susceptible to counter-attacks, particularly if they are somewhat slow in closing down the player with the ball. By committing players in the opponents half to win the ball, obviously fewer players are back in defense covering the vital spaces into which balls can be played.

The most difficult teams to counter-attack against are teams who play a very conservative low pressure defense where all five players retreat quickly into their defensive zone, thereby denying the opposition any space behind defenders into which balls can be played.

DELIBERATE BUILD-UP

The only effective form of attack against an opponent where all 5 players retreat into their defensive zone is a deliberate build-up out of the defense with the emphasis on keeping possession. The key factors in an effective build-up are:

1. Patience - In order to draw opponents out of their defensive zone it is essential a team is patient in its attack. It must attempt to draw opponents out of their defensive posture by keeping possession in the neutral zone.

2. Position changes - Interchanging of positions between teammates is essential in order to get free from tight marking and create space.
   a. For every position change at least 2 new paths are quickly opened up into which a pass can be made.
   b. The aim of position changes is always for one player to occupy the space opened up for him by another player.
   c. The ultimate success of a position change depends upon a correctly timed pass into the open area.

3. Mobility - In order to get free from man to man marking it is essential that players be mobile. Players must learn to show for the ball at the right time.
   a. When - Player must show for the ball when player with ball is ready to give it. If a player gets away from his opponent too early the opponent has a chance to catch up with him. If he shows for ball too late, element of surprise has been lost.
   b. How - A quick increase in pace or using some sort of disguise or feint with the shoulder.
      Checking runs - Feinting by taking a few quick steps in one direction before turning and sprinting in another. If a player wants the ball at his feet he can make space for himself by first running away from the ball, checking his run and then running back into the same space to receive the ball. Conversely, if he wants the ball played in front of him, he can first run to the ball, taking his opponent with him and then turning and sprinting after the ball which has been played behind the defender.

4. Once one or more opponents have been drawn out of the defensive zone and players are moving into open spaces, the emphasis must be on penetration and finishing with a shot on goal.

5. Improvisation. Players who have the ability to take opponents on 1 v 1 should be encouraged to do so in the attacking third of the field. Beating an opponent can result in a numerical superiority for the attacking team. Generally the time to take on an opponent 1 v 1 is when the defender has no teammate behind him providing cover.

6. Combination Play. One-two passes (wallpasses) and takeovers (when a player takes the ball from his teammate when he is being pressured by an opponent) are very effective ways of beating a packed defense.

OTHER INDIVIDUAL AND TEAM TACTICS

1. Learn to play quickly. Playing 1, 2, or 3 touch soccer in practice will teach players to think more quickly. Playing quickly means less running, therefore conserving energy. Remember, with indoor soccer there is less time and space, so players must learn to make decisions quickly while everything must be done at speed.
2. Don't dribble out of the defense while under pressure.

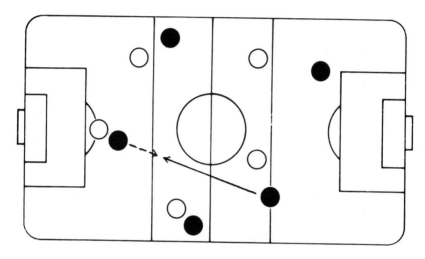

DIAGRAM 7
Example of creating width and depth in attack.

○ = Defender
● = Attacker

3. Create **Width** and **Depth** - In order to create space, the attacking team must strive to make the field wide and long. Width is obtained by having players going wide to the boards. By going wide, defenders are forced to follow their opponents, thereby creating space between them which can be exploited by the attacking team. Space can be created also in the length of the field. Forwards should strive to go deep into the opponents' half thereby forcing the opposing defenders back. Space is

hereby created in front of them into which balls can be played. When a team is bringing the ball out of its defensive zone, one or two forwards should push up to the opponents' red line and show for the ball from there. (see Diagram 7)

4. Play balls to player's feet or slightly in front of them so they can take the ball into their stride without slowing down.
5. In your own half of the field, run toward the boards. Avoid making square passes in your own half of the field.
6. If defenders make a run forward with the ball, they must not lose possession. An attacking defender must keep in mind the following:
   a. He must either get a shot off or make a good pass.
   b. After passing or shooting he must come straight back to his own position.
   c. Before making a forward run he must make certain there is a teammate in position to cover for him. If there is no one to provide cover the defender should stay back.
7. Always shoot across the goal mouth to the far post (see Diagram 8)

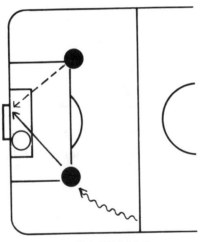

DIAGRAM 8
Far post passes and runs.

O = Defender
● = Attacker

TACTICS

ORGANIZATION

Webster defines organization as follows: "To arrange or constitute in interdependent parts, each having a special function or relation with respect to the whole." A soccer team is nothing more or nothing less than a collection of individual players. The success of a team depends upon the interaction between the skills and tactics associated with the game and how well each player understands his own duties and responsibilities vis a vis the rest of his team.

The importance of pre game organization cannot be over emphasized. Whereas coaches in the outdoor game are primarily spectators, the indoor coach is a direct participant in the outcome of the game. The old adage, if you're not prepared be prepared to fail is very true in indoor soccer. Through training sessions or team meetings every player must know what to do in specific situations. The following is a check list of items that should be part of the pre-game preparation.

1. **Line changes and substitutions**. A line is a unit of 5 players. A team will usually play with 2 lines. On the professional level one line is on the field for approximately 2 minutes. This is called a shift, i.e. a 2 minute shift. At the youth level the shifts are generally longer, perhaps up to 5 minutes. Indoor soccer and hockey are the only sports in which players may be substituted at any time without any stoppage of action. When the ball is in play substitutes can enter the game on the fly by jumping over the boards or entering the field through the gate. Substitutes may be used on an unlimited basis, provided the player substituted for is within the touchline of his own bench area or off the field of play within his own bench area before the substitution is made. Substitutions may also be made:

a. After a goal has been scored.

b. After a time penalty has been awarded.

c. On an injury timeout.

d. When the ball is out of play and has crossed the goalline or touchline over the perimeter wall.

e. After a team timeout.

A line change occurs when all five players are replaced by five new players. the best time for a line change is during one of the above guaranteed substitution occasions. Teams will be allowed 30 seconds to complete the substitutions. If, however, the time allotted for a shift has expired, teams must make a line change on the fly.

Line changes or substitutions are done by position. This way, each player knows exactly whom he is replacing. It is important that players remain alert while on the bench so a team is not caught short-handed or ends up with an extra player on the field during a line change.

HOW AND WHEN

A coach will decide when a line change is to be made. If the shift is about to run out during a guaranteed substitution time, a line change will then be made. If a coach calls for a line change on the fly there are certain guidelines that govern an efficient line change.

a. The team must have possession of the ball. Obviously it is foolhardy to have players run off the field when the opposition has the ball.

b. Ideally the change is made when the ball is in the attacking third of the field. However, if the opponent plays a low pressure defense the substitutions can be made in the team's own half of the field.

c. The player in possession of the ball should be alerted a line change will be made so he can hold the ball or make a safe pass to a teammate allowing time to complete the change.

d. Speed is of the essence in making an effective line change. Players must sprint to the bench and players ready to come on must sprint to their position.

At the professional level even the organization of the bench area plays an important role. If the bench area has two doors the forward players will usually come in through one door and defenders through the other door. Some innovative coaches at times have players coming off the field entering through one gate while their replacement exits through the other gate thus, for a while anyway fooling their opponents. Care must be taken that players coming off do not block players from coming on to the field.

Practice makes perfect and teams can ensure an efficient line change by making it part of their training sessions.

2. SPECIALTY TEAMS

   a. **Power play team** - At higher levels of play a coach will send a special unit of 5 players on the field when a team is in a man advantage situation, referred to as a Power Play. As soon as a time penalty is called by the referee, the special Power Play unit enters the field. When the Power Play has expired players must know which line will replace them. It could be for example that a player on the power play unit is also part of the next line going in. Instead of having players play two shifts in a row, one or more of the additional substitutes will take their place during the next shift.

   b. **Penalty Killing Team**- A special unit of 4 players must be selected whose job it is to kill a time penalty when the opposition has a power play. When the penalty has expired the players must know which line will replace the penalty killing unit.

3. 6th ATTACKER UNIT - If a team is behind late in the game, the coach may elect to pull the goalkeeper and replace him with a field player. A predetermined unit of 6 players will then enter the field with one of the field players designated as the goalkeeper. A different colored jersey is required.

4. SYSTEM AND STYLE - The coach must determine what system each line will play and whether they will play high pressure or low pressure.

5. RESTARTS - Teams must be prepared to select the right tactical solution during all set plays in attack and defense. Restarts are kick-ins, free kicks and corner kicks.

6. Scouting report on opposition.

   a. System and style
   b. Key players
   c. Individual matchups
   d. Defensive and attacking tactics
   e. Specialty teams
   f. Restarts

SYSTEMS OF PLAY

A system of play is the alignment of the 5 players on the field. The main criteria for selecting a particular system is that it must suit the players. For a system to be effective, it must be flexible, for during the course of the game the shape of the formation may vary.

Systems by themselves do not win games. No matter what system is employed, the principles of attack and defense are the same. In the final analysis it is the fitness level of the players, their technical ability and tactical knowledge that wins games.

Since the indoor game is played with 2 lines or units of players it may be necessary to play with 2 systems. The players dictate the system and obviously one system may suite one line better than another. Balance is probably the most important principle in deciding which 5 players should comprise one line. The 5 players should complement each other and there should be a good balance between attacking and defending players.

Simplicity is another important factor. Players must understand the system and the role of each player should be clearly defined. Yet at the same time a system should not be considered as a rigid harness, where players do not have the freedom to express themselves. There must always be room for improvisation and for individual actions, provided the players realize the time and place.

Even though the players usually dictate the system, sometimes a team will adjust its system to the opponent. For example, if a team is a heavy underdog in a game it may choose a system concerned primarily with not conceding goals.

There are 2 basic systems of play in indoor soccer, the 2-1-2 system and the 2-2-1 system.

2-1-2 SYSTEM - The 2-1-2 system provides for two defenders, one midfielder and two forwards. If a team is blessed with an over abundance of forwards it may elect to utilize this system. The primary emphasis of this formation is on attack. The two forwards are counted upon to score the goals. They should be very mobile, interchanging continually in order to get free from defenders. It is important that the two forwards do not play square. One should generally play in front of the other and when showing for the ball, one should show short and the other should show deep. (see dia #2).

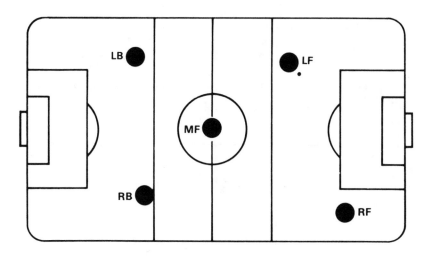

2-1-2 Formation

Positions
LB = Left Back
RB = Right Back
MF = Midfield
LF = Left Forward
RF = Right Forward

On defense the two forwards should immediately get goalside of the two defenders to contain them. This system is well suited for a team which prefers to play high pressure.

The **midfielder** in the 2-1-2 system is a link between his defenders and the two forwards. On attack he must show for the ball when his defenders have possession. Once in possession he becomes the primary playmaker of the team, distributing the ball in depth or width to his forwards. When the forwards are in possession he must give support from behind. He must also have a strong shot from distance.

On defense the midfielder must attempt to delay the opposition from attacking either by containing his immediate opponent or by picking up another opponent who has broken through.

The **defenders** have the primary responsibility of defending. They must mark their immediate opponent and give support. If the opponent plays with only one forward, one of the two defenders should push up to midfield. On attack the defender must provide support to his midfield player, and also be a target for an outlet pass from his goalkeeper. Should the defender go on an overlapping or attacking run he must make sure there is a player near him to take his place and there is space for him to run into.

2-2-1 SYSTEM - The 2-2-1 system provides for 2 defenders, 2 midfielders and one forward. (see dia #3).

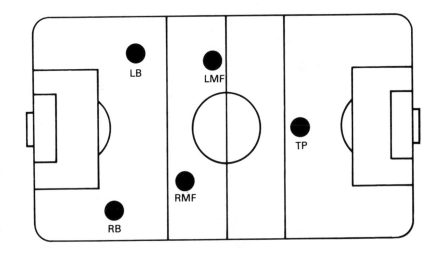

2-2-1 Formation

Positions
RB = Right Back
LB = Left Back
RMF = Right Midfield
LMF = Left Midfield
TP = Target Player

The **forward** player in a 2-2-1 formation is often referred to as a **target player**. He must be a strong and aggressive player capable of holding the ball under pressure. The 2-2-1 alignment lends itself to a team that likes to counterattack once it gains possession of the ball. The first target upon gaining possession should be the up front target player. The target player must be able to play with his back to the goal, thus screening the ball from the defender. The correct body positioning for screening the ball is a sideways one, while controlling the ball with the foot farthest away from the opponent.

When a ball is played into the target player's feet, he has several options. If marked tight he must have the ability to hold the ball until support arrives. He must also be able to turn quickly and get a shot off.

Because target players are closely marked by defenders they must have a keen sense to show for the ball at the right time in order to get free from their defender. The correct time to show for the ball is when the teammate in possession is ready to pass the ball. By showing too early, the defender is allowed time to catch up with the target player. Showing for the ball too late takes away the element of surprise and increases the chances of the pass being intercepted.

The target player can provide depth (making the field larger) for his team by staying up as much as possible thereby creating more space into which the ball can be played.

In the **midfield** it is important that the two players complement each other. For example if one player is attack-oriented the other player should be more defensively oriented. On attack they should provide support for the target player as well as one of them becoming an additional forward. As a general rule when one midfielder attacks, the other one provides support. When the ball is being brought out of the defense the midfielders must provide width by going wide to the boards.

Upon losing possession of the ball both players will attempt to get goalside of the ball and form the first line of defense.

The two **defenders** have the same responsibilities as under the 2-2-1 system. On attack however they may be more free to go on attacking runs since there are two midfielders in a position to cover instead of one.

FUTURE OF SYSTEMS - Undoubtedly variations of these two systems will evolve as the indoor game becomes more sophisticated. The evolution of the game will demand that future players be all-around players, capable of attacking and defending, and being able to play every position on the field. This can only be accomplished with players of exceptional skill, tactical understanding, good communication and endurance.

The one position on the field that may well revolutionize the game is that of goalkeeper. There is no place any more for goalkeepers incapable of playing with their feet. The future goalkeeper will be as adept with his feet as his hands. On attack therefore teams can establish a numerical superiority by the goalkeeper in effect becoming an additional field player.

SPECIALTY UNITS

Specialty units are specialized teams of players who enter the field during a time penalty. Generally a team will have a specialized unit of players when it finds itself in a man-down situation.

Close games are often decided by the effectiveness of the specialty teams. Choosing the right players for each unit and selecting the most efficient system are the key factors in determining the success of the specialty units. Once the players have been selected and a system of systems have been decided upon, both units must simulate game situations in their training sessions. Repetition is the mother of perfection and only by repeatedly practicing certain set plays will a team see the fruits of its labor. Specialty team practice should be a part of every indoor training session.

Discipline and concentration are two characteristics of effective specialty units. It is an absolute must players stick to the game plan and that they do not lose their composure under pressure. This is particularly true when a team is in a man down situation. Players must be careful not to commit another time penalty foul or the team will find itself minus two players.

POWER PLAY UNIT

I. FORMATIONS

In determining tne most effective alignment of its 5 players, a coach may have to design several combinations before coming up with one that works. Any system is good if it works. Simplicity is important. Ideally a team will employ no more than 2 or 3 formations. During the course of a long season, however, a team may be forced to change systems more frequently, as opponents may become familiar with certain game plans. Pages 87 and 88 show several power play formations.

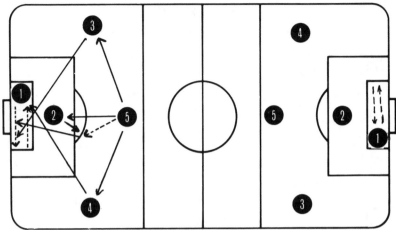

DIAGRAM 1

Note - *Player 1 must always show at the far post when either Player 3 or Player 4 has the ball. Player 2 must show for the ball and play wall passes with Player 5. Player 5 is the playmaker.*

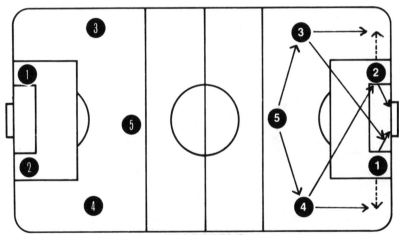

DIAGRAM 2

Player 5 is the key playmaker. He must attempt to commit a defender and then pass off to Player 3 or Player 4 who shoot across the goalmouth to either Player 2 or Player 1.

= Defender
= Attacker

POWER PLAYS

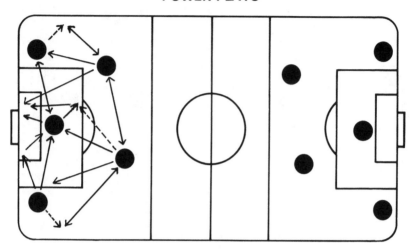

DIAGRAM 3

Instead of one playmaker on top, this system uses two players on top. Care must be taken, they are not caught square. Below are the passing options available. The key is to get the ball to player inside the penalty box.

II CHOOSING THE RIGHT PLAYERS

The best players for a power play are players capable of playing one touch soccer. Good ball control is a necessity. Players who need more than one touch to control a ball before passing it on should not be selected. The ball must be passed quickly from player to player until there is an opening for a shot. If a team plays with a point player (see diagram 1) he must be an excellent playmaker with good vision as well as having a good shot from far range. He is the key man in this type of alignment.

The players on the outside must possess a good shot. They must be able to kick a ball first time, without stopping it. They should be instructed to play balls across the goalmouth to a player positioned at the far post.

Players positioned near the goal must be quick to look for far post balls. Players who have a knack for "garbage goals" often do well in this position.

It would not be wise to employ 5 attacking players on the power play unit. When ball possession changes they must defend. Generally, two of the players must have good defensive abilities.

III KEY FACTORS
1. Keep the ball moving - Stopping the ball or dribbling slows down the attack, giving defenders more time to organize.
2. Keep possession - Control is the key to a successful power play. By spreading out and supporting at appropriate angles, defenders cover a larger area.
3. Be patient - The best plan is not to rush or become overanxious to score. Use the maximum time allotted if necessary to get a good shot. It is better to get one good shot off than 5 bad ones. A goal is a goal, whether it takes 15 seconds or two minutes.
4. Keep the shape of the formation intact - Players should strive to stay in their positions and not be drawn out. For example if the team loses possession of the ball but regains it, each player must return to his set position. Once the shape of the alignment changes, chaos can result.
5. Defending - Upon losing possession it is important to have a quick transition to defense. The opponent with the ball must be closed down immediately and the rest of the opponents must be marked man to man. By breaking out quickly, an opponent can score a short handed goal. There are teams who have become quite adept at scoring when they are a man down.
6. Penetrate - The objective of a power play is to draw the opponents out of their positions in order to get a shot off or make a penetrating pass to a player at the far post. Good vision and speed of action is vital if a team is to convert an opportunity into a goal.

PENALTY KILLING UNIT
A team that is unable to kill penalties effectively is very likely to lose. Close games are often decided by the effectiveness of the penalty killing unit.

I FORMATIONS
There are two basic alignments which teams can employ in killing off a penalty, although there are variations based upon the power play system of the opponent. One is called a box defense. The other one is called a diamond defense (see diagram 4). Teams should master both systems by simulating game conditions in their training sessions. It may be necessary to switch from one system to another during a game if one system proves ineffective.

PENALTY KILLING
FORMATIONS

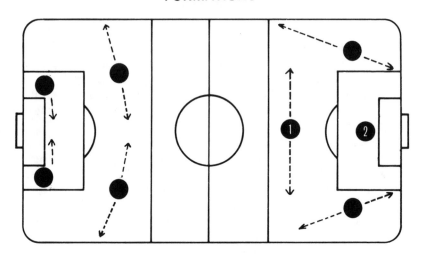

DIAGRAM 4

1. Box Defense —
Two front players must contain three opponents by switching back and forth, alternately picking up opponent's pointman and players on side.

2. Diamond Defense —
Player 1 must contain opponent's pointman as well as players on side.
Player 2 covers immediate area in front of goal.
Players 3 and 4 contain opponents on flank.

Whichever system is used, a team can either play a high pressure or low pressure defense. In a low pressure defense the 4 players on the man-down team will retreat into their defensive position immediately in front of their own goal.

Provided a team has the appropriate players and the system is well rehearsed in training, a high pressure defense can be very effective. Instead of withdrawing into their own defensive zone, the four players apply immediate pressure no matter where the ball is at the time. Some teams make it an objective to score on a man-down situation. In order to be successful there must be good coordination between the 4 field players and their goalkeeper. The goalkeeper in this system in effect becomes a defender thereby creating a 5v5 situation on the field.

II CHOOSING THE RIGHT PLAYERS

The best penalty killers are defensively-oriented players who are quick, with adequate ball control, good reflexes, a high work rate and cool heads. Discipline and concentration are requirements of an effective penalty killing unit. It is vitally important that the players stay in the same positions and that they are not drawn out. They must have the ability to read the offense and to react quickly and decisively in a disciplined manner.

Instead of using four defensive players, a team may elect to use one or two attacking players on its penalty killing unit. The attacking players should be the front two players on the man-down unit. Upon possession they must break quickly toward goal. Speed is an essential quality for these players.

III. KEY FACTORS

1. Overcommitting is an unforgiveable error when playing a man-down as it will result in the opposition temporarily having a two man advantage.
2. The defense employed in both systems is a zone defense. Obviously it is not possible to play man to man if the opposition has one more player. Each player is responsible for a certain part of the field within the defensive system.
3. When the penalty killing team gains possession of the ball it can do 1 of 2 things:
   a. Go for goal, particularly if the team is behind.
   b. Keep possession. A team cannot score if it does not have the ball. The longer the penalty killing team can keep the ball, the less time the opponent has to organize the power play.
   c. Clearing the ball down field, thereby running down the clock.
4. Upon gaining possession two players must stay in their own half. If three or four players attack at the same time a team leaves itself open to a counter-attack.

OTHER SPECIALTY UNITS

I. 6th ATTACKER - A team may elect to pull its goalkeeper and replace him with a field player, thus creating a numerical advantage of 6v5 on the field. Generally this occurs in the latter stages of a game when a team finds itself behind. One of the field players will be designated as the goalkeeper and must wear a goalkeeper's jersey.

The key player in this format is the designated goalkeeper. On attack he is the primary playmaker. He must possess good vision and be an excellent passer of the ball. At the same time he must be a more than adequate goalkeeper, for when his team loses possession of the ball he is the goalkeeper.

The success of this unit will in large part be determined by how much time is spent in training on 6v5 situations. If a team is able to tie the game it will generally return to its regular formation.

On the defensive side, teams must be prepared to counter the opposition's man advantage. It can elect to play either High Pressure or Low Pressure. The advantage of Low Pressure is that the opposition is denied space behind the defenders and the designated goalkeeper will be well out of his goal when attacking, leaving an inviting target once the team gains possession. On the other hand, playing a Low Pressure defense and by retreating into the defensive third of the field, the opposition is allowed to be within shooting range of the goal.

By playing High Pressure, a team can make it very difficult for the opposition to bring the ball out of their own half. By disrupting the flow of the attack in the opponents' half, a team might be able to convert a forced error into a goal scoring opportunity.

SUPER POWER PLAY - Another tactic a team can employ is to use a 6th attacker during a regular power play, thus creating a 6v4 situation. While obviously risky, the chances of scoring are great. Whether or not to pull the goalkeeper on a power play and replace him with a field player will depend on the score and the time remaining in the game.

High pressure is an effective tactic in winning the ball in the opponent's half.

Powerplay situations will often result in goals.

FIVE VERSUS THREE - If two time penalties have been assessed within two minutes, a team is forced to play minus two players. The man-down team in this situation should be primarily concerned with killing time and preventing the opponent from getting too many shots. Upon gaining possession it is best to clear the ball well into the opponents half of the field.

Note - When playing two men down there is no three line violation. See diagram 5 for an effective defensive alignment when playing two men down.

Other situations that can arise during a game are 4v3, 4v4, or 3v3 situations. By being adequately prepared teams can significantly increase their chances of winning.

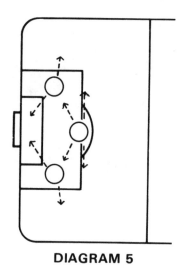

DIAGRAM 5

TACTICAL USE OF THE BOARDS

The most obvious element of the indoor game that separates it from the outdoor game is the boarding surrounding the field. The purpose of the boards is to keep the ball in play. During the early days of indoor soccer, the boards were seldom used for any tactical advantages. So, most teams played outdoor soccer indoors. However, as the game has become more sophisticated, teams have learned that they can use the boards to their advantage. In indoor soccer, the boards should be thought of as an additional player. There are 4 main ways in which the boards can be used to gain a tactical advantage:

1. WALL PASSES, also referred to as one-two passes. A wall pass in indoor soccer is an effective tool for getting around an opponent. Anytime a player is confronted by an opponent near the boards, one way to beat the opponent is to pass the ball against the boards in such a way that the ball will rebound behind the opponent. The player giving the pass will have run around his opponent on the opposite side ready to collect the ball in stride.

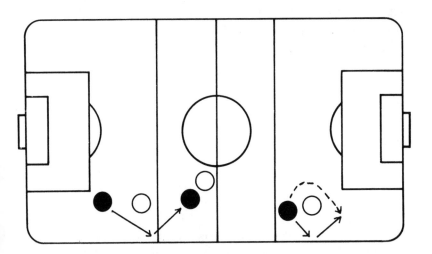

O = Defender
● = Attacker

2. PASSING BALL TO A TEAMMATE. Making a wall pass to a teammate gives a player another passing option. The boards provide an additional opportunity to pass to a player who might not otherwise be a target.
3. NEAR POST SHOTS - Near post shots are shots aimed at the boards within two yards of the near post. The tactical objective is to have a teammate score on the rebound. These are very difficult balls to deal with for goalkeepers. When an opponent shoots on goal from the side, the first rule for a goalkeeper is to make certain not to get beat at the near post. When the ball rebounds off the boards, next to the goal he must quickly readjust his position in order to deal with a potential shot from straight on.

It is important for the team in possession that when the near post shot is taken, a player runs on to the ball at the right time. He should not arrive too early and wait for the ball since he will undoubtedly draw an opponent.
4. PLAYING BALL OVER THE TOP AGAINST THE GLASS OR BOARDS - This is a tactic sometimes used by teams who have difficulty getting behind the opponent's defense. Basically it involves lofting the ball over the heads of the defenders, off the plexiglass and then running on to the rebound. An alternative is to shoot the ball between the defenders off the boards and again running on to the rebound.

SET PLAYS

There are certain occasions during a game where a team has the opportunity to execute a set play. These instances are commonly referred to as restarts. They occur during stoppages of play resulting from corner-kicks, free kicks (direct and indirect), goalkicks, kick-ins and kick-offs. Many goals are scored from well-executed set plays. Corner-kicks and free kicks provide the best opportunity to score from a set play. The key to successfully converting a set play into a goal is to keep it simple.

Don't forget the element of surprise. Once an infraction has been called there is no second whistle to restart play. Quite often a quick pass to an open teammate is more effective than a set play which takes time to organize. Sometimes players are so concerned with executing a particular set play that they do not see the obvious. A quick pass should always be the first option.

Generally a team should rely on no more than two or three set plays, or perhaps one set play with several options. During a long season it may be necessary to come up with new plays. To be successful, players must comprehend the set play and spend time rehearsing the various moves during each training session. In order to eliminate confusion it is best to appoint one player who will decide which particular set play to use. It is also advisable to have two players on the ball the moment a foul is called so one player can make a short pass to a teammate.

Defending against restarts is as important as devising a set play for attack. Each player's responsibility must be clearly defined. Against free kicks in and around the penalty box defenders will generally choose to set up a wall. The goalkeeper must decide whether or not to set up a wall. In indoor soccer defenders must be 10 feet away from the ball. Care must be taken not to line up closer to the ball. Encroachment is considered a serious offense and can result in a two minute penalty.

It is important not to tie up too many players in a wall. The more players comprising a wall, the fewer players there are remaining to mark opposing players. Generally two players in a wall is sufficient, unless perhaps the opposing team has an indirect free kick within the penalty box immediately in front of the goal. When lining up the wall the goalkeeper must make certain he can see the ball. By having too many players in the wall the goalkeepers vision may be obstructed.

Note - If a wall is employed it should always consist of the same players. Also, do not put the best defenders in the wall. In defending against corner kicks it is vital to cover the most dangerous area, that in front of the goal. The defenders must attempt to block the passing lanes into the penalty box. Generally one or perhaps two players should line up ten feet from the ball. This prevents the opposition from shooting balls against the boards, thus taking an option away and making the pass more predictable.

Coaches who are well prepared will have scouted the opponents' restart tactics and come up with suitable counter tactics.

One point of caution is that teams are often most vulnerable to get scored upon after an attacking set play. Care must be taken therefore not to commit too many players into the attack.

PHYSICAL FITNESS

Fitness training must reflect the demands of the game. The indoor game consists of short sprints, with and without the ball, quick starts, stops, and sudden changes of direction. Obviously the more fit the player, the better he will be able to execute his overall skills and play to full potential.

Most fitness training should be done with the ball. This is particularly true for players under the age of 16. Coaches must design exercises that incorporate physical conditioning, technique and tactics. The exercises listed in the sections dealing with dribbling and passing, particularly the section on Technical/Tactical exercises incorporate all three of these elements.

Coaches of younger players should be concerned with technique, improving the player's ability to read the game, and to make quick decisions. To emphasize physical fitness, coaches can demand that ball exercises be performed at speed with many repetitions and with little rest in between.

Basically the indoor game is a form of interval training. On the pro level players play for two minutes and rest for two. Interval training therefore is the most effective method to get players physically fit to play the indoor game.

Interval training consists of work or exercise followed by a properly prescribed rest interval. The relief interval avoids excessive production of fatigue products. The key to success in interval training lies in utilizing the proper intensity of exercise, followed by a rest interval. Initially the work to rest ratio is 1:3, but gradually it is increased to 1:2 or even 1:1.

The interval training program is designed around the concepts of sets. A set is a group of work and relief intervals. There are a certain number of repetitions within each set and each repetition is performed over a certain training distance and within a specific amount of time.

Most of the exercises listed in the Passing and Dribbling section can be performed on an interval basis. For example, a passing exercise can be performed at high speed for 1 minute duration. The players rest for 1 or 2 minutes and then perform the same exercise again. They do 6 repetitions, which equials 1 set. After the completion of one set the players may rest up to 3 minutes or more and then go on to the next set. The longer the exercise and the more strenuous it is, the longer the relief interval must be. Instead of complete rest, the relief interval can consist of an easy technical exercise (i.e. passing while standing still or juggling).

Eventually teams should lead up to high intensity workouts of three minutes, followed by a three minute rest. If a player can go all-out for three minutes in training he certainly will be able to go all-out during a two minute shift in a regular game.

Speed training over short distances should be part of a fitness program. Quickness off the mark should be stressed. Particularly true in indoor soccer, the first yard or two is the most important. Players must be able to explode from a standing or jogging position. Many speed exercises can be done in conjunction with the ball. No matter what specific fitness exercises, the ball should always be the focal point.

CONCENTRATION AND DISCIPLINE

Indoor soccer by its nature is an emotional game. Its fast pace and intensity can unnerve even the calmest coach. Concentration and discipline are therefore of the utmost importance.

Concentration implies focusing all of your attention on the game. All great athletes have great concentration. Lack of concentration results in anger, frustration, emotional outbursts and temper tantrums. All of these are distractions which tend to crowd a player's attention when instead his attention should be focussed on the game. Players who lack self control and composure usually end up committing fouls which result in time penalties. The better you concentrate, the better you will play. Players as well as coaches must learn to shut everything out which might distract them from the game.

Discipline is an important concept in indoor soccer, primarily because it is such a highly organized game. It is vitally important that players know their roles and responsibilities and that they stick tothe "game plan". Lack of composure on the part of players or coaches will obviously disrupt the game plan. By setting a high standard for himself and controlling his emotions the coach will undoubtedly influence his players to do the same.

GLOSSARY

CHIP PASS - A high lofted pass over head of a defender to a teammate.

CLOSING DOWN - Pushing up on an opponent when ball possession changes.

COMBINATION PLAY - Passing between two or more players as they move to the opponents' goal.

CORNER KICK - A direct free kick taken from the corner spot by a member of the attacking team after ball goes out of bounds over back wall, and was last touched by a defender.

COVERING - Providing support to a teammate challenging for the ball.

COUNTER-ATTACK - A team's quick attack toward the opponents' goal after winning possession of the ball in its own half.

DEFENDERS - Players whose main function is to prevent goals.

DIRECT FREE KICK - A kick awarded to a team for a serious foul by the opponent. Teams may score goal directly, without ball having to touch another player.

FINISHING - A shot resulting in a goal.

FORWARDS - Players whose primary function is to score goals.

GOALKEEPER - The only player on the field who may use hands (in penalty area) and whose primary function is to prevent balls from going into the goal.

GOALKICK - A kick taken from anywhere in the goal area after the ball went out of bounds over the boards and was last touched by an attacking player.

HIGH PRESSURE - A form of defense geared toward winning the ball in the opponent's half of the field once possession is lost.

INDIRECT FREE KICK - A kick awarded to a team for less serious fouls by the opponent. Goal can only be scored after ball has been touched by two players.

KICK-IN - The method of putting the ball back into play after it has gone out of bounds over the side boards.

LINE - A unit of 5 players

LINE CHANGE - Substituting one line of players with another line either on the fly (during game) or during a stoppage of play.

LOW PRESSURE - A form of defense. When ball possession is lost, all 5 players withdraw into their own half or defensive third of the field.

MARKING - Closely guarding an opponent.

MAN TO MAN DEFENSE - A form of defense where each player must closely guard an opponent.

OVERLAP - The action of a defender who comes from behind and goes on an attacking run past his midfield or forward players.

PENALTY KICK - Direct free kick taken from penalty spot. It is awarded after a member of the defending team commits a serious infraction within their penalty box.

SPECIALTY TEAMS - Specialized units of players who enter the field during power play, man down situations or sixth attacker situations.

SET PLAY - A predetermined attacking maneuver employed in restart situations (free kicks, corner kicks, kick-ins).

SIXTH ATTACKER - Tactic generally employed in latter stages of game where team will pull its goalkeeper and replace him with an extra attacking player.

SHIFT - The amount of time a unit of players is on the field.

SUPPORT - Moving into open positions when a teammate has the ball, thereby providing him with several passing options.

TRANSITION - The ability of a team to convert from attack to defense and the reverse.

TACKLE - The method of dispossessing an opponent of the ball by use of the leg or foot.

TARGET PLAYER - A forward player whose main function is to provide a far target to his teammates.

THRU PASS - A pass which penetrates the defense.

WALL PASS - When under pressure of an opponent, passing the ball to a teammate, then running around the opponent for the return pass. Also called "give-and-go."

ZONE DEFENSE - Form of defense where each defender is responsible for guarding opponents in a particular area of the field.

HOW THE INDOOR GAME IS PLAYED

The **FIELD** is approximately 200 feet long and 85 feet wide and is artificial turf. Dasher boards, topped by plexiglass, surround the field. Players' benches and penalty box are behind the dasher boards at mid-field.

The **BALL** is the standard leather ball, 27-28 inches in circumference, weighing 14-16 ounces.

The **GOAL** is 6-feet, 6-inches high and 12-feet wide and is set into the boards at both ends of the field.

THE PLAYERS AND OFFICIALS

A **GOALKEEPER** and **FIVE FIELD PLAYERS** for each team are usually on the field together.

FREE SUBSTITUTION — players change while the flow of the game continues. Any number of substitutions may be made during a game.

POWER PLAYS — A team will play one (or two) men short if the referee cites a player for a serious foul or if a player is guilty of delay of game or ungentlemanly conduct or when a penalty kick is awarded. (More information under Basic Rules.)

ACTIVE ROSTER will include 20 players, 16 of which may dress for a game.

A three-man **OFFICIATING** system will again be utilized in the 1985-86 regular season. The system will place the Senior Referee and Referee on the field of play with the Assistant Referee off the field of play.

THE BASIC RULES

The **GAME** is played in four 15-minute quarters. There is a three-minute interval between the first-and-second and third-and-fourth quarters and a 15-minute halftime. The clock stops when a goal is scored, the ball leaves the playing area, a penalty kick, penalty call, red line violation, an official timeout, or with any whistle by the referee. The clock restarts with the official's hand signal and the playing of the ball.

The visiting team will have possession for kickoffs in the first and third quarters; the home team in the second and fourth.

Play restarts (after the ball leaves the playing area) with a kick-in at the touch line where the ball left the field area.

Each team is allowed one time-out per half. However, if a team shall not have used its second half time-out, such team shall be allowed a single one-minute time-out in the overtime period.

GOALS are scored when the entire ball crosses the goal line.

PENALTIES are called and time served in the penalty box for serious fouls, delay of game, ungentlemanly conduct (two minute penalties) and violent conduct (five minutes and ejection). The penalty call will not be made and play stopped until the guilty team gains possession of the ball or play otherwise is over.

Minor Infractions are penalized by an Indirect Kick. The ball must be touched by another player other than the kicker before entering the goal.

Major Infractions are penalized by a Direct Kick and — depending on how serious the foul — time in the penalty box. A goal can be scored from a direct kick. Two-minute penalties are also called if 1) a player deliberately puts the ball over the perimeter wall and out of play; 2) too many men are on the field; 3) defending players line up closer than 10 feet for direct or indirect kicks and encroachment is called; 4) if players take longer than five (5) seconds to take a free kick after having been signalled to do so by the referee.

A **Penalty Kick** is awarded to a team when a defender INTENTIONALLY commits a major offense against an attacker in the penalty area (25' x 30'). The penalty kick is taken from the penalty spot (24' directly in front of goal). All players except the designated kicker and goalkeeper must stay outside the penalty area and the restraining arc.

RED LINE VIOLATION is called when a forward pass crosses both red lines (60 feet apart at mid-field) in the air without being touched by another player. Change of possession and an indirect kick from the center of the red line restarts play.

CORNER KICKS are taken if ball leaves playing area between the two flags on the goal line having been last touched by the defending team.

INDOOR CONDENSED LAWS

From The Official Indoor Soccer Rules, United States Soccer Federation

LAW 1 — *Field of Play:* Approx. 200 ft. long by 85 ft. wide.
Perimeter wall: 3 ft. 6 in. to 4 ft. 6 in. high, fully enclosing area topped by plexiglass.
Goal: 6 ft. 6 in. high by 12 ft. wide.
Goal area: 16 ft. wide by 5 ft. from the goal line.
Penalty area: 30 ft. wide by 25 ft. from the goal line.
Corner spot: 9-in. diameter.
Center spot: 9-in. diameter
Center circle: 10-ft. radius.
Red lines: 30 ft. from center line across field width, each half.
Markings: Minimum 3 in., maximum 5 in. wide.
Center line: Indicated by a white line across field.
Touch line: Broken line from corner spot to corner spot on both sides of the field at a distance of 3 ft. from the perimeter wall.

LAW 2 — The Ball: circumference (27-28 inc.) and weight (14-16 oz.) same as in outdoor soccer.

LAW 3 — Number of players: Maximum of 16 may dress; Maximum of 6 per team on field at anytime and minimum of 4; Time penalty is delayed if it would reduce a team below 4; Substitutions may occur on an unlimited basis and "on the fly" provided a player leaving the field arrives at the touchline at his bench before his replacement enters the field. Play will be held up to allow substitutions after a stoppage for a goal, time penalty, injury or after the ball has left the field. During "guaranteed substitutions" teams shall be allowed thirty (30) seconds to complete all player substitutions.

LAW 4 — Player Equipment: Consists of a shirt, shorts, socks and flat-soled or indoor shoes. Goalkeeper must wear colors which will distinguish him from all other field players and referees.

LAW 5 — Referees: Three referees — Senior Referee and Referee on the field, responsible for control of the game; an Assistant Referee stationed at the timekeeper's bench to call three-line and substitution violations.

LAW 6 — Other Game Officials: Timekeepers operate the time and scoreboard details and the time penalties under the referee's jurisdiction. One attendant in each penalty box. Goal Judges indicate whether the whole ball has crossed the goal line for a goal.

LAW 7 — Duration of the Game: Four quarters of 15 minutes each, with one 15-minute halftime interval and two 3-minute quarter intervals. The clock stops on every referee's whistle and starts upon a signal. Each team is allowed 1 time-out per half. If the game ends in a tie, fifteen-minute sudden death periods are played until a winner is decided.

LAW 8 — Start of Play: The visiting team has first possession in the first and third quarter; the home team in the second and fourth quarter. The home team has decided in advance the direction to attack in the first quarter. Teams change direction at each quarter interval.

LAW 9 — Ball in and out of Play: The ball is out of play when it passes over the perimeter wall, when a goal is scored, or when the referee stops play. The ball is in play at all other times, even if it rebounds from the referee, perimeter wall, goalpost, surrounding plexiglass, etc.

LAW 10 — Method of Scoring: A goal is scored when the whole of the ball passes completely over the goal line, providing no infraction has been committed by the attacking team.

LAW 11 — Red Line Violation: It is a violation if the ball is passed forward by any member of the attacking team so that it passes over two red lines in the air without being touched by any other player (of either team). If this happens, the referee will award an indirect free kick to the opposing team, to be taken at the center point of the first red line crossed by the ball. It shall not be considered a three line violation if a team is two men down.

LAW 12 — Fouls and Misconduct: A player who intentionally kicks, trips, strikes, boards, jumps at, pushes, holds, violently charges, or charges in the back of an opponent, or who intentionally handles the ball (except the goalkeeper), shall be penalized by a direct free kick. Any one of these offenses committed in the penalty area by a defender will result in a penalty kick for the offensive team and a two-minute penalty to the offender. Any of these offenses judged to be very serious by the referee regardless of their location shall be penalized by a two-minute penalty against the offender. A player guilty of a second penal offense in any game shall receive a caution. The third such penalty shall result in a mandatory ejection. A player guilty of intentionally causing the ball to leave the field of play or the indirect offenses of obstruction, dangerous play, legal charging not in playing distance can also be awarded a two minute penalty. However, this is not a penal offense.

If a non-playing personnel (coach, trainer, gm) is guilty of ungentlemanly conduct or conduct likely to bring the game into disrepute or such other miscounduct he shall be issued a caution (yellow card) or ejection (red card) but no time penalty shall be served by any player for a non-player's misconduct. The referee shall report the misconduct to the appropriate authority for disciplinary action.

If a player is guilty of violent conduct (or serious foul play) he shall be ejected (red card) permanently and must retire to the dressing room. He may be replaced by a substitute but the substitute must go into the penalty box and serve a five-minute penalty before entering the game. Players shall be released after one powerplay goal is scored in cases of ejection.

Goalkeeping Restrictions: If the goalkeeper delays action by failing to distribute the ball to another player or play the ball outside the penalty area within five seconds of having received the ball; if a defender passes back to the goalkeeper from another zone and the goalkeeper plays the ball with his hands; if the goalkeeper handles the ball, after putting it down to be played, prior to the ball being touched by an opponent, an indirect free kick will result.

Penalty Against Goalkeeper: When a two-minute penalty is awarded against a goalkeeper, it shall be served by another field player.

Power Play Return: If one team is reduced by penalties to fewer players on the field than its opponents and the team having more players scores a goal, then the player who has served the most of his penalty time can return to the game. Only one penalized player may return on each goal.

Shootout Attempt: The referee may award a shootout attempt if, in his opinion, a player on the defending team intentionally commits a penal offense in his team's defensive third of the field and outside of the penalty area which prevented an attacking player from a reasonable goal scoring opportunity.

Delaying Restart of Play: The referee shall award a blue card of unsportsmanlike conduct and a two-minute penalty to a player, who, in the opinion of the referee, engages in tactics which delay the restart of the game.

Cumulative foul count: Upon the accumulation of a club's sixth (6th) non-time-penalty foul and multiples of six (6) thereafter (ie. 12, 18, 24, etc.) during any quarter or overtime period, the referee shall award a two-minute bench penalty against the offending team for persistent infringement of the Law.

LAW 13 — Free Kicks: Classified into two categories — direct from which a goal can be scored directly against the offending team, and indirect, from which a goal cannot be scored unless the ball has been touched by a second player before entering the goal. A team will have five seconds to take a free kick once signaled to do so by the Referee.

LAW 14 — Penalty Kicks: Awarded for offenses committed by defenders against an attacker in the penalty area. The kick is taken from the penalty spot (24 feet from goal line) by any player on the offended team. The goalkeeper must stand on the goal line and between the posts. All players except the kicker and goalkeeper must be outside the penalty area. The ball is in play as soon as it is kicked forward one-half rotation.

LAW 15 — Kick In: The ball is put back into play with an indirect free kick, with the ball being placed on the touchline at the point nearest where it went out of play.

LAW 16 — Goal Kick: When the ball completely crosses over the perimeter wall at the goal line between the two corner flags after being last touched by a player from the attacking team, it is put back into play by a kick from the goal area by the defending team.

LAW 17 — Corner Kick: When the ball completely crosses over the perimeter wall at the goal line between the two corner flags after being last touched by a player from the defending team, it is put back into play be a kick from the corner spot on the side of the field the ball had left. The corner kick is a direct free kick for the attacking team.